747·7 GRE

THE L[~~~]

HOME DESIGN WORKBOOKS

KITCHEN

HOME DESIGN WORKBOOKS
KITCHEN

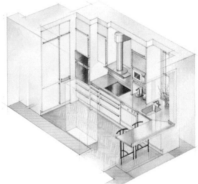

JOHNNY GREY

G^E

For Harry, Felix, Augusta and Benedict – who may find it useful someday.

Project Editor BELLA PRINGLE
Project Art Editor COLIN WALTON
Picture Research JULIA PASHLEY
Location Photography PETER ANDERSON
Studio Photography MATTHEW WARD
Stylists MICHELLE AND YVONNE ROBERTS
Production Controller ALISON JONES
Senior Managing Editor MARY-CLARE JERRAM
Managing Art Editor AMANDA LUNN

First published in Great Britain in 1997 by
Dorling Kindersley Limited
9 Henrietta Street, London WC2E 8PS
This edition published in 2000 for Greenwich Editions

A member of the Chrysalis Group plc

Copyright © 1997 Dorling Kindersley Limited, London
Text copyright © 1997 Johnny Grey

4 6 8 10 9 7 5 3

www.dk.com

A CIP catalogue record for this book
is available from the British Library

ISBN 0 8628 8317 2

Text film output in Great Britain by Optigraph
Reproduced in Singapore by Pica
Printed and bound in China by L.Rex Printing Co., Ltd.

INTRODUCTION · 6

ROOM PLANS · 48

PLOT YOUR DESIGN · 74

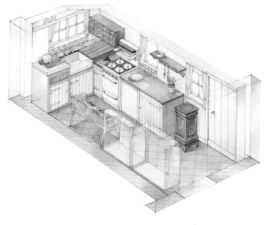

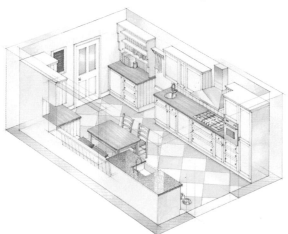

CONTENTS

INTRODUCTION

△ **DISTINCTIVE SURFACES**
Hand-crafted details, such as this wood door with its "suitcase" handle and inlaid surround, contribute to the atmosphere of a kitchen.

FOR MANY OF US, the kitchen is the most fused room in the house. It is not just a refuelling station, but the place where adults congregate and children naturally migrate, and not just for food but company.

I recall with great affection, the small, chaotic family kitchen in our London house where my mother cooked for the seven of us, and where we ate most meals. Although the kitchen was very cramped, low-ceilinged, and dark, and contained a gigantic, noisy fridge that took up about a quarter of the space, mealtimes were memorable

for their animated conversations and laughter. To my mind, too few kitchens seem to be able to combine successful planning with the warm atmosphere I remember from my childhood.

Reconciling practical considerations, such as where appliances and furniture should be placed so that they are efficient to use, with comfort is hard, but they are the mainstay of ergonomic design. In *Kitchen*, I have tried to show you how to achieve a balance that works for you, whether you are designing a brand-new kitchen from scratch or simply remodelling an existing one.

CREATIVE SPACE ▷
The lived-in appearance of Elizabeth David's kitchen was a source of inspiration to me. Through her, I discovered that kitchens could be comfortably furnished, like any other room in the house.

◁ **CROCKERY STORAGE**
Keep an open mind when
choosing kitchen elements.
A cupboard for storing
crockery may be more in
keeping with your design
than fitted kitchen units.

appliances, cabinets, and other fittings that look
attractive in catalogues and showrooms but do
not suit your lifestyle or cooking habits. "A good
meal is never expensive but a bad one always is."
So the saying goes, and it is these costly mistakes
that I intend to help you avoid.

The three major expenses when installing a
kitchen are furniture, appliances, and building
work. It is important to assess your budget and
decide which expenses should be given priority.
In my opinion, it is better to have fewer pieces of
furniture made to a high standard, with perhaps
a make-do cupboard that can be removed at a
later date, than a complete kitchen made from
cheap, low-quality units that will not last.

KITCHEN ACTIVITIES

Start by deciding what you will be doing and
how much time you want to spend in your new
kitchen. Do you want to use it just for cooking
the occasional meal, for professional cooking, or
would you like it to be the main family room in
the house? I've found many of my clients prefer
kitchens that contain not only a cooking area
but an informal dining area, where adults can
entertain and children can do their homework,
draw, or paint. They also request a "soft" area

△ **STAINLESS STEEL**
Think carefully before
selecting a kitchen cabinet
finish. An industrial material
such as this is heat- and
water-resistant, and reflects
light, brightening the room.

Having been involved in kitchen design for the
last 18 years, and having come into contact with
the needs of many individuals and families, I
have developed a great deal of affection for the
kitchen as well as knowledge about its design.
Early on, much of this enthusiasm came through
the influence of my late aunt, the cookery writer
Elizabeth David. She was the person who first
pointed out to me that kitchens do not need to
be plastic laminate boxes, carefully arranged
around the perimeter walls. Her kitchen was
highly atmospheric, almost a study (she wrote
many of her books at its scrubbed pine table)
but also a living room, and all this at a time
during the 1950s and 1960s when its design
was completely out of step with the fashion.
Today, we have come full circle. Our idea of
the kitchen as a place to live in, relax, and be
sociable, as well as cook, would have pleased her.

Designing a kitchen is usually the biggest
financial investment after buying a house or flat,
and it is all too easy to be seduced into purchasing

with a carpet for
children to play on,
a sofa and television
for relaxation, and a
kitchen desk for
dealing with home
administration and
telephone calls.

COOL STORAGE ▷
Consider a larder for storing
fresh produce rather than
relying solely on the fridge.

◁ UTENSIL RACK
A wrought-iron rack above a hob or food preparation area offers easy access to kitchen utensils. It also makes an attractive display.

In order to produce a successful kitchen design that matches your needs, you have to go back to fundamentals. First establish what you enjoy and what you dislike about your existing kitchen, and use the ideas (*below*) to help build up a picture of your ideal kitchen. Consider how you move about the room: how far do you have to travel from the fridge to the food preparation area? Are storage cupboards difficult to reach?

Are worktops close to the hob? Is it easy to carry in shopping bags from the car?

Once you have worked out how you are going to use the space, research the features that best suit your needs. In the chapter featuring *Kitchen Elements*, the pros and cons of the major kitchen appliances are outlined. For example, if you cook with plenty of fresh ingredients you will be able to judge whether a pantry cupboard or a family-

△ GLASS SPLASHBACK
As an alternative to tiles, consider using glass to protect walls near worktops.

WHAT DO YOU WANT FROM YOUR KITCHEN?

Before committing yourself to expensive furniture and equipment, assess your lifestyle and the kind of non-cooking activities you wish to undertake in your new kitchen. Use the following options to help you decide what sort of kitchen will suit you best.

❶ A ROOM SOLELY FOR COOKING MEALS WITHOUT INTERRUPTION.

❷ A FAMILY ROOM WHERE LIGHT MEALS ARE EATEN.

❸ A KITCHEN THAT DOUBLES UP AS A DINING ROOM.

❹ A SPACE FOR PROFESSIONAL CATERING ON A LARGE SCALE.

❺ A ROOM FOR RESEARCHING, WRITING, AND PLANNING MENUS.

❻ AN AREA WHERE CHILDREN CAN PLAY AND DO HOMEWORK.

HOW SUITABLE IS YOUR ROOM?

Before you decide to spend a lot of money on remodelling an existing kitchen, or on designing one from scratch for a new home, make sure that the room you choose to be the kitchen has the necessary features or can be easily adapted.

☐ Is the total space big enough for you or your family's needs? Could the room be extended?

☐ Does the room have access to other associated rooms such as the pantry, utility room, and dining room? Is it possible to add or move the doors in order to improve the link?

☐ Is the room adjoining the garden so that you can have an outdoor dining area in summer, watch while your children play, or keep the door open for extra ventilation?

☐ Does the room under consideration have easy or direct access to the garage or parking area for unloading shopping?

☐ Is the natural light good? Could lighting be improved by adding a new window?

☐ Are there enough electrical and plumbing points, and are they well distributed?

sized fridge is a better investment. Whatever the dimensions of your kitchen, try to limit the number of elements to keep the plan simple. In small kitchens, durable items that offer multi-purpose functions may be better than specialized features that have only an occasional use. The same applies to small gadgets and electrical appliances whose limited purpose may not justify the amount of space they occupy.

KITCHEN CHARACTER

The personality of a room is determined by the individual elements. In kitchens, these elements also have to be functional because they are used more intensively than other household furniture, and come into daily contact with heat, steam, and water. Stainless steel fridges and worktops, for example, contribute an air of professionalism to the domestic kitchen as this highly durable

material is frequently used in restaurant kitchens. Wood cupboards, on the other hand, or cooking utensils hanging from racks, provide the warm atmosphere associated with country kitchens.

It is not only kitchen appliances that matter. Other details, such as your choice of worktops, lighting, cabinet finishes, wallcoverings, and flooring, all present an opportunity to influence the character of the room and contribute to a comfortable kitchen environment. When choosing these elements, bear in mind both aesthetic and practical considerations. Kitchen flooring, for example, needs to be hygienic, hardwearing, and "soft" underfoot, as well as beautiful to look at, while a well thought-out mix of task lights and soft, ambient lighting can make all the difference to working and eating areas. For kitchen cabinets, the quality of craftsmanship and choice of materials are vital

QUALITY FINISHES ▷
Try to buy the best quality cabinets you can afford. Good craftsmanship is a sensible investment as it ages particularly well.

WHAT COULD YOU CHANGE?

Use the following checklist to help you pinpoint what it is about your kitchen that you would like to improve or replace.
☐ Change shape of existing room.
☐ Alter architectural features.
☐ Improve access to natural light.
☐ Reorganize layout of kitchen cabinets.
☐ Upgrade major appliances.
☐ Increase number of electrical points.
☐ Redesign lighting.
☐ Relocate plumbing.
☐ Rationalize available storage space.
☐ Rethink the size and height of worktops.
☐ Change worktop materials.
☐ Replace flooring.
☐ Renew wallcoverings and splashbacks.
☐ Alter style of cabinets and door handles.
☐ Rehinge entry doors.
☐ Change furniture.
☐ Update all curtains, blinds, cushions, and other soft furnishings.
☐ Decrease noise levels.

ALTERING THE SHAPE ▷
To create a large family kitchen with space for a sitting, dining, and desk area, three smaller rooms have been combined.

if they are to withstand daily wear and tear. Also, by choosing from a range of gloss or matt, pale or dark, cabinet finishes, you can affect how the cabinets reflect natural light in the kitchen room.

KITCHEN LAYOUT

For me, kitchen planning tends to fall into two categories, fitted and "unfitted". Fitted kitchens, developed in the 1950s as the "dream" solution to kitchen design, rely upon units being placed against the walls, while unfitted types use a variety of freestanding elements to furnish the room.

The "unfitted" approach particularly interests me, and it is an area of kitchen planning that I pioneered throughout the 1980s. It has grown in

popularity, as for many individuals the warm, comfortable appearance of unfitted kitchens is both easier to live with, and work in. The Family Kitchen (*below*), is an example of this planning. By grouping all the cooking and preparation facilities together, fewer elements have to be placed around the walls, leaving space for a table, a sofa, and doors opening out onto the garden.

Above all, the purpose of this book is to explain how to arrive at an ergonomic kitchen design where the user feels comfortable. Whether your kitchen is large or small, it will help you to choose appliances and furniture according to your needs, and arrange them for ease of use, in a way that is not only practical but looks wonderful.

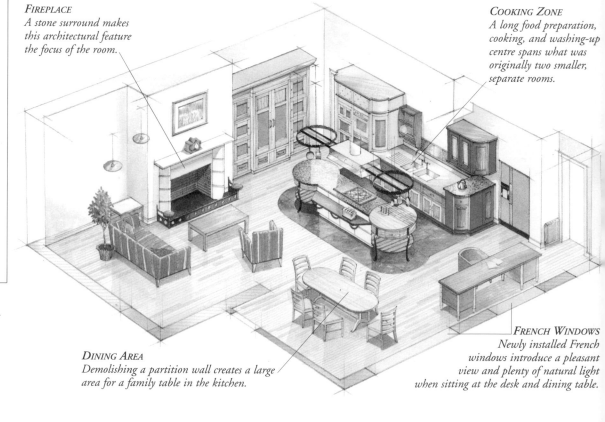

FIREPLACE
A stone surround makes this architectural feature the focus of the room.

COOKING ZONE
A long food preparation, cooking, and washing-up centre spans what was originally two smaller, separate rooms.

DINING AREA
Demolishing a partition wall creates a large area for a family table in the kitchen.

FRENCH WINDOWS
Newly installed French windows introduce a pleasant view and plenty of natural light when sitting at the desk and dining table.

PLAN OF ACTION

Before you go ahead with your alterations, use this checklist to ensure that you have not overlooked any requirements. A date for completion and good coordination of plumbers, electricians, and fitters is also important. Consider the following:

☐ Have you received permission from relevant authorities for structural alterations?

☐ Can you afford the time to do some of the work yourself?

☐ Will you need professional help?

☐ Have you estimated the costs accurately and allowed a little extra?

☐ Have you left enough money for finishing decoration and fixtures?

☐ Is this amount of work within your budget or are you happy to keep some features as they are?

☐ Will your plans increase the resale value of the property?

☐ Have you made other plans for eating when work is in progress?

◁ **KITCHEN AFTERCARE**
A finished kitchen needs regular maintenance to keep it looking its best. Here, wood worktops have been oiled, wood floors varnished, and cabinet doors repainted.

ASSESS YOUR NEEDS

THE FOLLOWING questions will help you to focus on your specific kitchen needs, and think about ways to approach kitchen planning so that, as you work through the book, you will be able to compile a list of the kitchen elements and designs that suit you best.

STORAGE

The number of people you cater for, how many meals you cook at home, the type of foods you use, how you shop, and who needs access to storage, determine the type and amount of storage space you need in your kitchen.

■ FOOD:
□ Do you cook with a mixture of fresh, frozen, chilled, dried, preserved, or tinned foods, or does one type predominate?
□ Do you have enough fridge, freezer, and cupboard space to house your preferred choice of cooking ingredients?
□ If you cook with mainly fresh ingredients, do you have cool, well-ventilated storage for vegetables etc., or do you rely solely on the fridge?
□ If you like to prepare meals well in advance and freeze them, do you have enough storage space in your freezer?
□ Do you work all day, live far from the shops, or are without a car so that you need more than the average amount of storage space?
□ Do you buy essential items in bulk and need additional space to keep large packets, tins, and bottles?
□ Do you store bottles of good wine and so need an even temperature site away from the oven and hob?
□ Are your food storage facilities, such as the fridge and larder, within a few steps of food preparation areas to save journeys across the kitchen?
□ Are items of food well-organized so that they are easy to find, not lost or forgotten at the back of kitchen cupboards?
□ Do you expend unnecessary energy reaching up to pick cooking ingredients off high shelves, or bending down to reach into units below counter level? If so, could you reorganize your storage cupboards more efficiently so that frequently used items are kept somewhere between knee height and eye level?

□ If you have young children, do you want some high storage areas to keep certain rationed foods, such as sweets and biscuits, out of reach?

■ EQUIPMENT:
□ Have you accumulated a huge amount of kitchen equipment that needs storing? If so, have you sorted out the equipment to check that every item is useful?
□ Are there any less frequently used items, such as an ice-cream maker, that could be kept out of the way on high shelves?
□ Have you allowed room to store everyday food preparation equipment within reach of food preparation worktops?
□ Is there space for heavy food processors, toasters, and juicers to be kept plugged in at the back of countertops?
□ Can cooking utensils be stored close to the hob counter?
□ Can cutting boards and knives be stored within reach of food chopping areas?
□ Can pans and baking trays be stored near the oven?
□ Are your day-to-day plates, glasses, and cutlery stored close to the eating area for table laying, or close to the dishwasher?
□ Have you allowed space to store non-food associated items such as cleaning and shoe-polishing products, in the kitchen?

FOOD PREPARATION

An efficient workspace for food preparation needs careful planning. Think about its location in relation to other activity areas, the type of food you prepare, the amount of people you cook for on a daily basis, and whether you need extra preparation areas for others to share the work.

□ How much day-to-day wear are your food preparation worktops subjected to? Do you prepare several meals at home daily, or do you often eat out? Do you cook for just yourself, for you and your partner, or do you have a family to feed?
□ Do you prepare food on your own, or does your partner or children share the work and space with you? If children are involved in food preparation, would a low-level worktop be useful?
□ Do you cook with mainly fresh food that requires lots of preparation space, or a high proportion of convenience foods that require minimal preparation space?
□ Would you like worktops made from different materials to suit different cooking activities, such as a cool, smooth slab of marble for pastry-making? Or, would you prefer the same surface material throughout the kitchen?
□ Are you a sociable cook and prefer facing into the room while you work? Or, do you prefer facing the wall, or looking out of a window while you prepare food?

COOKING

Your preferred style of cooking, be it elaborate cuisine for entertaining, or quick reheating of convenience food, whether you are a solitary or sociable cook, how frequently you cook at home, and the number of people you regularly cook for, determine the type and location of cooking appliances.

☐ Do you want to face into the room while working at the hob? If so, consider a centrally placed cooking area.
☐ Would the type of hob cooking you enjoy benefit from an easy-to-control fuel, such as gas or induction?
☐ Would a wipe-clean ceramic hob surface make kitchen cleaning less of a chore?
☐ If you enjoy gourmet cooking, would you benefit from a hob fitted with extra features, such as a barbecue grill?
☐ Would an extraction system be useful to help dispel cooking smells? If so, would a permanent or retractable hood be more suitable in the space above the hob?
☐ Do you regularly cater for more than five people? If so, is your oven big enough, or would a double oven or heavy-duty range be more suitable?
☐ Would you like to have the capacity to prepare, reheat, or defrost meals in an instant? If so, have you allowed space to accommodate a microwave oven?

EATING

Think carefully about the sort of meals that you would like to eat in the kitchen, whether just breakfasts and snacks, or lunches and suppers, the number of people that sit down to eat at any one time, and how often you entertain. These decisions will help you determine the size and type of table you need, plus the dimensions and best location of the dining area.

☐ Do you want to eat in the kitchen or would you rather eat in a separate room?
☐ What meals do you specifically want to eat in the kitchen?
☐ How many people do you want to be able to seat on a day-to-day basis?
☐ Do you want to entertain in the informal surroundings of the kitchen?
☐ Have you planned the location of the table so that it has a good source of natural light, is draught-free, and sits away from the main kitchen activity areas?
☐ Would a foldaway table or small corner table be more suitable if space is limited?
☐ Would a bar eating area around a central island be sufficient?
☐ Would a built-in window seat or banquette rather than chairs help you fit more seats around a table?
☐ Is a hardwearing tabletop an important requirement?

WASHING-UP AND WASTE DISPOSAL

Make washing-up and food recycling simple by choosing the sink, drainage space, and dishwasher on the basis of the amount of work you have to do.

■ WASHING-UP:
☐ If you use a large quantity of plates and glasses on a daily basis, is it worthwhile investing in a dishwasher to save time? If the dishwasher is going to be on while you are in the kitchen, have you checked that it has a quiet operational noise level?
☐ If you use many large pans, do you have a big enough sink to be able to wash them up properly?
☐ While washing-up, do you want to face the wall or have a window view, or perhaps face into the room?

■ WASTE:
☐ Will you dispose of all kitchen waste, or are you going to recycle some of it?
☐ Do you have the space in the kitchen to store recycling bins for items such as newspapers, bottles, and cans, or will they be stored outside, or in the garage?
☐ Would you like to store food waste for a compost heap? If so, have you a bin next to the preparation area for food scraps?

HOW THIS BOOK WORKS

THIS BOOK explains the practical know-how you need to design a room that matches your lifestyle and create an efficient and comfortable living space; it will help you plan a brand-new kitchen or adapt an existing one. A series of questions helps you assess what you want from your own kitchen, then a survey of appliances and fittings guides you to elements that best suit those needs. Next, three-dimensional plans of six kitchens explain how to engineer a successful design, and finally, instructions on measuring and drawing up a kitchen plan leave you equipped to translate ideas into reality.

2. SELECT FITTINGS ▽

To help you compile a list of the features that will best suit your needs, a range of appliances and fittings are surveyed (*pp.16–47*). A "Remember" box draws your attention to the key design points, and the pros and cons of each element are discussed. Where the height of a fitting or appliance may have some bearing on how easy it is to use, a small diagram recommends ideal dimensions and the most efficient operational height.

1. IDENTIFY YOUR NEEDS ▽

A number of preliminary questions (*pp.12–13*) are asked to encourage you to think about your kitchen needs, and the condition and potential of your present kitchen. By examining aspects of your lifestyle that you take for granted, such as how you cook, eat, and wash up, you will find it easier to identify the most suitable appliances and most appropriate design solutions for remodelling your kitchen or building a new one.

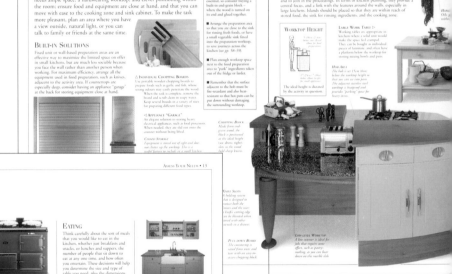

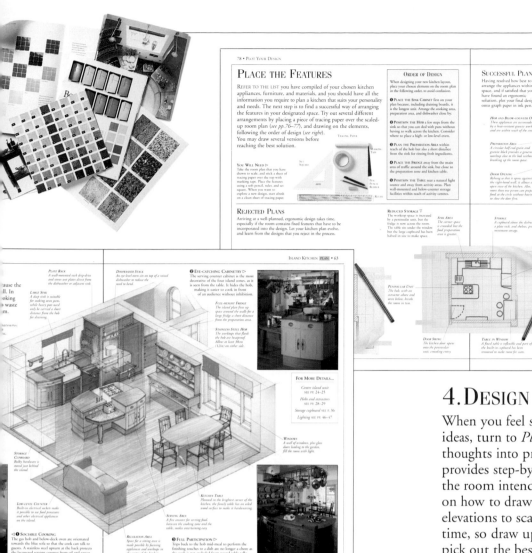

4. DESIGN YOUR KITCHEN △

When you feel satisfied with your own kitchen ideas, turn to *Plot the Design* and put your design thoughts into practice (*pp.74–81*). This section provides step-by-step instructions for measuring the room intended for your kitchen, plus details on how to draw the floor plan and different wall elevations to scale. Arriving at a solution takes time, so draw up variations on tracing paper, and pick out the best elements from each.

3. LEARN HOW TO PLAN △

A chapter on *Room Plans* (*pp.48–73*) looks in detail at six existing kitchen designs and offers advice and inspiration on how to bring together all the elements in your own plan. A three-dimensional drawing, a bird's eye view plan, photographs, and a list of design points, explain the thinking behind each design solution.

HOW TO USE THE GRAPH PAPER

■ Draw up your room to scale (*see pp.76–77*) using the graph paper provided (*pp.89–96*). You may photocopy it if you need more.

■ For a kitchen with small dimensions, use the graph paper with a metric scale of 1:20, where one large square represents 1m and one small square represents 10cm. Therefore, an area 60cm long is drawn as six small squares. Alternatively, use the imperial scale of 1:24, where one large square represents 1ft and a small square 3in.

■ For a room with greater dimensions, use the graph paper with the smaller scale of 1:50. Again, the large squares represent 1m and the small squares 10cm. Alternatively, use the imperial graph paper with the scale of 1:48, where a large square equals 4ft and a small square 6in.

■ With the room drawn on graph paper, try various designs on a tracing paper overlay.

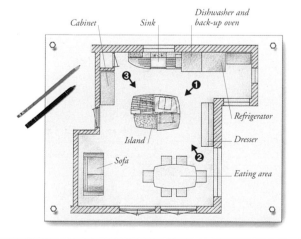

Cabinet Sink Dishwasher and back-up oven

Refrigerator

Dresser

Island

Sofa

Eating area

KITCHEN ELEMENTS

FRESH FOOD STORAGE

IF YOU COOK with a lot of fresh produce, try to plan well-ventilated storage facilities set away from hot, steamy areas of the kitchen, rather than becoming wholly dependent on the fridge. To avoid unnecessary wastage and for a healthy turnover, ensure all fresh supplies are visible.

LARGE STORAGE

A pantry cupboard is the modern-day solution to the walk-in larder. Its generous storage capacity allows you to house all your foods – with the exception of those that are kept in the fridge-freezer – in one location rather than at a variety of sites above and below the worktops. A successful larder cupboard has shelves with adjustable heights to meet the demands of modern packaging, and a shallow depth so that items at the back do not disappear.

SHALLOW SHELVES
Avoid over-filling the door shelves with heavy items or they may be difficult to open.

TOP SHELF
Less frequently used items, or those that you have bought in bulk, can be stored at this less accessible height, out of sight.

MODERN LARDER △
A storage cupboard with sliding, fold-back doors allows maximum visibility and accessibility, while requiring the minimum clearance when opening. Stainless steel racking shelves allow air to circulate within; walls, floor, and doors are easy to clean.

PULL-OUT DRAWERS
Fresh vegetables, bread, or large goods can be placed in compartments below waist height.

PANTRY CUPBOARD ▽
An attractive piece of furniture that stands away from the main traffic, this cupboard offers cool, dark, well-ventilated storage for a wealth of fresh and non-perishable produce. Half-depth shelves keep items in reach and prevent them from becoming lost and forgotten.

FULL-HEIGHT DOORS
Doors of this size reveal the entire contents of the cupboard when open.

GRANITE SHELF
A cold granite shelf 60cm (24in) deep, keeps cheese and other fresh produce at room temperature.

REMEMBER

■ Work out in advance which foods you prefer to keep in the pantry cupboard and which in the fridge-freezer. If you buy in bulk, you will need additional storage areas in the kitchen.

■ When choosing a pantry cupboard, the central shelf should be about 60cm (24in) deep, while access to mid-height shelves is easiest if these shelves are 15–30cm (6–12in) shallower than the central shelf.

■ If you intend to store a lot of fresh produce in the cupboard, ventilation ducts to the outside may improve conditions. The pantry needs to be dark inside to slow down the deterioration of fresh fruit and vegetables.

STORAGE HEIGHT
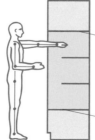

Ideally, the top shelf should sit at eye level.

Low shelves should be widely spaced or become drawers to house large items.

The most accessible storage area sits between knee height and eye level. Store items rarely used above and below this line.

SMALL STORAGE
Certain fresh foods, such as tomatoes, eggs, soft fruits, and baked foods, are damaged by cold refrigeration and taste best if kept at room temperature. Here are some modern and traditional solutions to this problem.

△ **BREAD-BIN DRAWER**
This space-saving alternative to a traditional bread crock has a lift-out drawer for removing crumbs. The wooden lid can double up as a cutting board.

REVOLVING RACK ▷
A modern rack provides dark, well-ventilated conditions to store root vegetables.

MEAT SAFE ▽
A traditional meat safe, with its netted doors, is good for keeping flies off fresh food, while allowing ventilation; central heating and warm summers limit their use to eggs, cheeses, various soft fruits, and tomatoes.

WIRE-MESH DOORS
These keep household dust and insects off fresh foods.

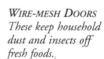

RAISED HEIGHT
A meat safe on legs ensures that food is stored above floor level.

CHILLED FOOD STORAGE

WHEN JUDGING WHICH fridge or freezer best suits your needs, bear in mind the size of your family, your shopping and eating habits, and the position the appliance will occupy in the kitchen. How you organize your food in the space available is the key, so check that the model of your choice has adjustable shelves and see-through drawers to offer the most flexibility.

UNDERCOUNTER FRIDGE-FREEZERS

In a small kitchen, consider an undercounter, side-by-side fridge-freezer that will keep limited worktop space free for food preparation. If the appliance is flush-fitting, the interior space is well-organized, and the appliance is placed directly below a food preparation area, it can work very efficiently. Bear in mind though, that the fridge is one of the most-used items in the kitchen, and frequent bending down to take out or put back food may become irritating.

FRIDGE INTERIOR
Ensure the space inside caters for tall items, such as bottles.

SMALL FRIDGE-FREEZER ▽
Think carefully before deciding to buy a small fridge-freezer. If you enjoy cooking on a regular basis, you may find its limited capacity very inconvenient.

DOOR SHELVES
Store short-term frozen items here, for easy access.

FRIDGE DRAWERS ▽
A recent innovation in cold food storage is fridges and freezers that are compact enough to fit into the space of a drawer. These allow chilled fresh produce to be stored at a number of strategic sites around the kitchen.

EASY ACCESS
Large fridge doors can be difficult to open; single pull-out drawers offer easier access.

FRESH PRODUCE
This section varies between 0.5°C (32°F) and 3°C (37°F), with 50 per cent humidity.

HIGH HUMIDITY
In this drawer, a relative humidity of up to 90 per cent keeps fruit and vegetables fresh and crisp.

REMEMBER

■ Before choosing a chilled storage system, consider how often you prepare and freeze meals in advance. Or does your cooking focus on fresh foods?

■ Other features that may influence your decision are: CFC content, noise level, defrost capability, and energy efficiency rating.

■ When placing your fridge within the room, leave space for access. Specify which way you want the door to hinge, and plan a worktop nearby for loading and unloading food.

■ After a shopping trip, beware of packing the fridge too tightly with food as it takes time to return to a cool temperature.

FREESTANDING MODELS

Designed to stand alone as a kitchen feature, these appliances are not limited by the need to fit within standard cabinetry. Many models sit on wheels and can be easily moved for servicing or to a new location.

DAIRY COMPARTMENT
A transparent lid protects the contents from taste and odour transfer.

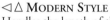

◁△ **MODERN STYLE**
Handles the length of the door (*above*) make it easy for adults and children to open the large stainless steel fridge, and gain access to the well-organized contents in easy-clean plastic and glass compartments (*left*).

SPILL-SAVER SHELVES
Raised shelf edges help to contain spills.

DEEP DOOR SPACE
Large items can be stored two-deep, while a high side prevents tall cartons from toppling out.

▽ **TRADITIONAL STYLE**
If you prefer your fridge to be unobtrusive, consider housing it within a cabinet. Vegetables that need ventilation but not refrigeration can be stored in open-weave baskets below.

VENTILATION
Vents at the front enable the unit to have a coil-free back so that it can be fitted flush with the wall.

FRUIT DRAWER
Located in the coolest part of the fridge, see-through fruit and vegetable drawers allow you to see exactly what needs replacing or throwing out.

NON-PERISHABLE FOOD STORAGE

ORGANIZATION OF, and access to, store cupboard supplies is paramount, but because tinned, bottled, and dried foods have fewer environmental needs than fresh foods and location-sensitive appliances, one option is to keep them in slim units and corner carousels that can fill up leftover spaces in the kitchen.

NARROW SOLUTIONS

In larger kitchens, tall, dual-sided pull-out cupboards are an efficient option because items at the back can be easily accessed. Make sure there is room on either side to reach into the pull-out, and that there is a mid-height "fence" to prevent articles from falling out. Place less regularly used, heavier items, on the bottom shelf.

EASY OPENING
A centrally placed handle distributes the weight, making the unit lighter to open, even when it is full.

CLEARANCE HEIGHT
Allow space between each shelf for the easy retrieval and return of taller items.

DIRECT ACCESS
Drawer runners are an integral part of the fence rail, so that access to the shelves is uninterrupted.

TALL BOTTLE STORE
Space for tall bottles is created by removing the penultimate shelf divider.

CAPACITY
Each shelf is deep and wide enough to hold at least four large bottles.

BOTTLE SAFETY
The rail holding bottles in place is thicker for these heavier items.

LAMINATE FINISH
Hardwearing laminates are easy to clean and will withstand knocks.

◁ PULL-OUT STORAGE
The success of this store cupboard lies in its flexibility and ease of access. The door slides open and is nudged closed, while shelf heights and compartment sizes can be altered to suit a variety of non-perishable produce.

BOTTLE PULL-OUT △
A narrow, below-counter pull-out is useful for cooking oils, vinegars, and cooking wine. It can be tucked into a narrow space adjacent to the hob, oven, or preparation area.

OVER-COUNTER UNITS

Wall-mounted cupboards and racks provide storage space over countertops. They can be useful for stationing spices, oils, and wine, if placed within reach of the food preparation area. In small kitchens where space is at a premium, over-counter units may be the answer, but in order to function ergonomically they should sit at eye level. This height can be a problem because the cupboard may block your view of the counter when working, and also pin your head and shoulders back. For this reason, try not to place cupboards above heavily used worktops or the sink cabinet.

TOP SHELF
Least important jars should be stored on high shelves.

SHELF DEPTH
The shelves should be between 15–30cm (6–12in) deep so that all items are visible.

CHICKEN-WIRE DOOR
A fabric-backed wire door allows air to circulate whilst protecting food items from direct sunlight.

WALL FIXTURE
Ensure wall brackets are securely mounted as the unit is extremely heavy when full.

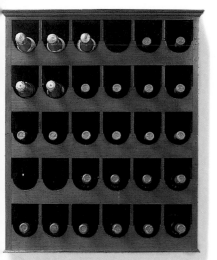

CONDIMENT CUPBOARD ▷
Depending on how tall you are, place the cupboard at a height somewhere between 1.8–2.2m (5ft 10in–7ft 2in). Allow a gap of at least 45cm (18in) between wall units and the worktop below.

◁ WINE RACK
Consider storing your selection of wines on a wall rack to free up floor space. Do not position the rack too close to the oven because wine favours an even temperature around 15.5°C (60°F).

CORNER IDEAS

Even in very small kitchens where space is precious, the corner area where worktops meet is often neglected. This "dead" space can be turned into a useful storage area if a pull-out mechanism is fitted below counter-level. Alternatively, plan a body-height carousel to fit neatly into a corner space, and bridge the gap that may be left between an eye-level oven and a food preparation worktop.

OPEN CAROUSEL
Fixed doors revolve around a pivot and swing shut into place.

REAR SECTION
Once the front section has been pulled out, the rear section slides forward, out of the deep corner space.

◁ BODY-HEIGHT CAROUSEL
Rather than having to delve inside a dark corner cupboard, the doors of this unit fold back to offer access to its contents. Jars, tins, and packets are neatly arranged on four shelves that revolve when nudged. Standing 2m (6ft 6in) high, no effort is required to reach the top shelf.

◁△ TWO-PART PULL-OUT
Contemporary kitchen manufacturers have responded to the challenge of kitchen storage needs by tailoring units to fit into awkward corners. In this two-part unit (*left and above*), frequently used non-perishable foods, such as pasta and noodles sit in the front section (*left*), while items stored in bulk are kept at the back, and can only be accessed once the front unit has been swung to the side (*above*).

FOOD PREPARATION

TO ENSURE COOKING IS enjoyable, the chopping and preparation area needs ample space, a hardwearing worktop, and clever positioning within the room; ensure food and equipment are close at hand, and that you can move with ease to the cooking zone and sink cabinet. To make the task more pleasant, plan an area where you have a view outside, natural light, or you can talk to family or friends at the same time.

BUILT-IN SOLUTIONS

Fixed unit or wall-based preparation areas are an effective way to maximize the limited space on offer in small kitchens, but are much less sociable because you face the wall rather than another person when working. For maximum efficiency, arrange all the equipment used in food preparation, such as knives, adjacent to the activity area. If countertops are especially deep, consider having an appliance "garage" at the back for storing equipment close at hand.

△ INDIVIDUAL CHOPPING BOARDS
Use portable wooden chopping boards to prepare foods such as garlic and fish, whose strong odours may easily penetrate the wood.
When the task is complete, remove the board and scrub clean in soapy water. Keep several boards in a variety of sizes for preparing different food types.

◁ APPLIANCE "GARAGE"
An elegant solution to storing heavy electrical appliances, such as food processors. When needed, they are slid out onto the counter without being lifted.

CLOSED STORAGE
Equipment is stored out of sight and does not clutter up the worktop. This is a useful feature to include in a small kitchen.

(see pp. 58–59)

ROLLER SHUTTER
A roll-up mechanism saves space as it does not open outwards like a cupboard door.

CONCEALED SOCKET
Wall sockets inside the "garage" mean appliances are always plugged in, ready for use.

VISIBLE STORAGE
Spices and pulses are attractively displayed in clear bottles and drawers for ease of use.

▽ MINI PREPARATION AREA
A small food preparation centre provides enough space to store knives, seasonings, and spices within easy reach of the activity area.

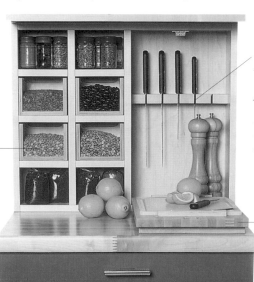

CHOPPING BLOCK
Made from end-grain wood, the block is positioned at the ideal height (see above right); slots in the wood hold sharp knives.

KNIFE SLOTS
A holding system that is designed to protect both the knives and the user; a knife's cutting edge can be blunted when stored with other utensils in a drawer.

PULL-DOWN BOARD
The countertop is saved from wear and tear with an easy-to-access chopping block.

REMEMBER

■ Chopping is the primary activity in food preparation. A good chopping surface is essential, so consider buying a built-in end-grain block – where the wood is turned on its end and glued together.

■ Arrange the preparation area so that you are close to the sink for rinsing fresh foods, or have a small vegetable sink fitted into the preparation worktop, to save journeys across the kitchen (see pp.58–59).

■ Plan enough worktop space next to the food preparation area to "park" ingredients taken out of the fridge or larder.

■ Remember that the surface adjacent to the hob must be fire-retardant and also heat-resistant so that hot pans can be put down without damaging the surrounding worktop.

Freestanding Preparation Centres

A central island unit or work table provides a focus in the middle of the room dedicated to food preparation. These freestanding features *(right and below)* enable the cook to face into the space as he or she works and to join in the proceedings. In terms of kitchen planning, they provide a central focus, and a link with the features around the walls, especially in large kitchens. Islands should be placed so that they are within reach of stored food, the sink for rinsing ingredients, and the cooking zone.

Hanging Rack
Oils, garlic, and cooking utensils are stored within reach of the preparation area.

Worktop Height

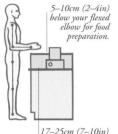

5–10cm (2–4in) below your flexed elbow for food preparation.

17–25cm (7–10in) below elbow-height for small appliances.

The ideal height is dictated by the activity in question.

Large Work Table ▷
Working tables are appropriate in kitchens where a solid unit would make the space feel cramped. They can be bought as individual pieces of furniture, and often have a platform below the worktop for storing mixing bowls and pans.

Hob Area
The hob is set 15cm (6in) below the worktop height so that you can see into pans. The adjacent stainless steel worktop is heatproof and provides "parking" space for heavy items.

Serving Area
A free surface for resting plates of food, between the hob area and a kitchen table, makes serving easy. Crockery can be stored in the cupboard below.

◁ Island Unit
An island arrangement helps to concentrate key activities into a small area so the cook does not waste time and energy moving about the kitchen. The island is divided up into zones for different activities. The activity determines the worktop height, size, and also material for each zone.

Low-level Worktop
A low counter is ideal for jobs that require some effort, such as pastry-making, as you can bear down on this marble slab.

FOOD RINSING AND WASTE DISPOSAL

HYGIENIC AND WELL-PLANNED food and waste management are essential to a well-run kitchen. Consider a sink with two basins, where fish, meat, vegetables, and fruit can be cleaned without interrupting other kitchen activities that require water, such as pan-filling. Plan convenient sites beneath food preparation centres for organic waste collection, and storage bins for collecting bottles and cans away from the main activity centres.

FOOD-RINSING SOLUTIONS

In large kitchens, where the distance between activity zones is greater, a second sink for washing food, close to the preparation area, may be convenient. Alternatively, plan a double sink unit, where food can be rinsed in one half and utensils, pans, and crockery washed in the other.

△ SMALL RINSING SINK
Choose a worktop sink that is large enough to be useful. Place it close to the edge so that you do not have to lean across the worktop to use it, and ensure it is well sealed to prevent leakage into units below.

SPLASHBACK
A high stainless steel guard protects the wall from water splashes.

SPRAY-RINSING HEAD
An extendable spray attachment, for cleaning fresh ingredients, is linked to the water supply by a flexible hose.

◁ DOUBLE SINK
A double sink enables two people to stand at the sink at once and perform different tasks. As the sink is used intensively, it is manufactured from durable, water- and rust-resistant material, such as stainless steel.

DOUBLE BASIN
Use one sink to rinse fresh ingredients and the other to soak dirty pans and dishes.

FRONT PANEL
A stainless steel panel prevents water from dripping onto the wood cabinet below.

MULTI-PURPOSE SINK ▽
A well-designed, deep single sink can sometimes offer more flexibility than a double unit with two small sinks. A large sink can accommodate baking trays and pans, while a colander, draining rack, and chopping board can be slotted into the sink to divide up the internal space as required.

DRAINING RACK
Water drains directly into the sink. A separate plate rack or draining board is no longer necessary.

WASTE DISPOSAL
Flush food scraps washed off plates down into the waste disposal unit fitted beneath the waste outlet.

SINGLE TAP
Shift the tap to the left or right, depending on the task in hand.

COLANDER BASKET
Drain rinsed foods and t replace the basket with th chopping block, stored be

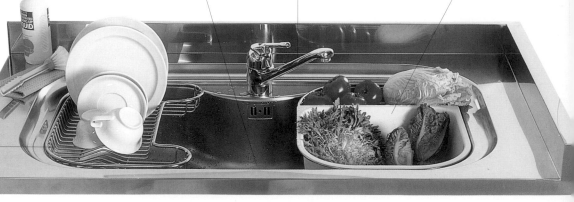

WASTE RECYCLING

Households generate huge quantities of waste materials, much of which can be sorted out and stored for recycling. Before allocating space to recycling in your kitchen, contact the local authority to establish the categories of rubbish that they accept. If you have a garden, consider organic waste.

ODOUR-FREE BINS
Wash out bottles and tin cans before storage, or they will smell.

◁ **STACKING BINS**
Lightweight plastic bins can be easily stacked on top of one other, while lift-up flaps allow the quick deposit of items. Allocate one bin for each category of recycled waste. Store the bins out of sight and plan to empty them regularly.

△ **ORGANIC WASTE HOLE**
A hole or slot carved out of a wood worktop feeds directly into a waste bin below, and is an efficient way of clearing away organic waste matter, such as vegetable peelings. As well as keeping the worktop free, the waste matter can be tipped directly onto a garden compost heap.

△ **RECYCLING COMPARTMENTS**
Here, a pull-out drawer adjacent to the sink holds two recycling bins. Avoid shallow bins that have to be emptied frequently. Make sure the bins are easy to lift out, and that the drawer interior can be wiped clean. Also, check that the drawer is sealed to prevent odour transfer.

REMEMBER

■ Plan organic waste bins or a waste disposal hole close to the food preparation area, to avoid having to transport food scraps across the kitchen.

■ The size of rubbish bins for household waste needs to be in keeping with the size of your family. Emptying a bin several times a day, especially if you live in a block of flats, may become annoying.

■ If you are unhappy about separating out waste materials for recycling, try to recycle just "clean" waste; newspapers and glass bottles are the easiest and cleanest to separate out and store in stacking bins for weekly recycling.

WASTE DISPOSAL

For those who live in small flats or houses, recycling may not be an option because of the space needed to sort out and store the different materials. A waste compactor occupies a small amount of space and will compress all bulky household rubbish into tight bundles. Alternatively, consider a waste disposal unit to dispose of food scraps. A less expensive option is a slim, free-standing pedal bin.

◁ **ELECTRIC COMPACTOR**
All household rubbish is fed in and then compacted at the turn of a switch. This small unit does not need emptying for several weeks at a time.

CHARCOAL FILTER
The filter reduces odours when the door is open.

PEDAL BIN ▷
A flexible unit, as it can be transported to wherever you are working. Its slim shape takes up less floor space than other pedal bins.

PLASTIC BOARD
This creates an extra chopping block above the sink. Organic waste can be swept directly into the waste disposal unit.

WASTE-FREE SINK
Waste does not interfere with sink drainage as it is fed directly into the waste disposal system.

▽ **WASTE-DISPOSAL UNITS**
If you do not intend to recycle organic waste, consider a sink fitted with an electric waste disposer. This feature will grind down food scraps and bones into paste and then wash them away. It can be noisy when the grinder is switched on.

"PARKING" AREA
Place washed items here that are awaiting preparation.

BATCH FEED
The waste disposal unit fits into this section. A safety plug is turned on to start the electric grinder.

HOBS AND EXTRACTORS

THE POSITION AND CHOICE of hob is crucial to the enjoyment and efficiency of the kitchen. Ideally, it should face into the room, have a sink nearby, parking space suitable for resting hot pans, and, wherever possible, a high-performance, well-designed, powerful extractor for removing cooking odours and steam. Task lights built into the extractor hood will help light the hob area.

COMBINATION HOBS

A worktop-mounted gas, halogen, or induction hob and a wall-mounted electric oven offers flexibility of fuel types – quick response from the hob, and even-temperature oven cooking. The variety of hobs has become increasingly specialized. Manufacturers now offer components such as steamers, griddles, or wok burners, so that you can build up hob features to suit your cooking style.

REMEMBER

■ In the life of your kitchen, much cooking time is spent standing at the hob. Arrange your kitchen plan accordingly by placing the hob in a safe, sociable, and convenient location, perhaps forming the central feature in an island arrangement (*see pp.62–63*).

■ When planning a site for your hob, bear in mind the limitations of extractor systems, required to expel steam and cooking smells. Extractors work best when connected to outside walls; hobs on islands require more powerful systems.

■ British and US manufacturers rate extractors according to how many cubic feet per minute (CFM) of air they can process. Work out the volume of your room, to determine the rating you need.

■ A hob must be easy to clean to work efficiently. Many pan grids are now designed to fit into a dishwasher. Check that the rest of the hob is simply designed so that grease cannot collect in awkward corners.

■ Beware of unstable pan grids. If the prongs are short or stand high of the hob, saucepans may accidentally topple off the grid.

■ If your cooking habits demand constant use of the hob, ensure the hob floor and pan grids are made from heavy-duty materials; stainless steel and vitreous enamel are highly suitable.

GAS HOB WITH GRIDDLE ▽

A solid, semi-professional range can be fitted with a combination of different components that suit your cooking habits. Here, a powerful down-draught extractor sits between a griddle and four gas rings.

GAS BURNERS
Cast alloy pan grids surround the two gas burners.

PAN SPACE
A stainless steel surface between the grids avoids overcrowding when four large pans are on the hob.

GRIDDLE PLATE
This flexible system enables food to be grilled on the hob rather than in an oven.

INBUILT EXTRACTION
Food odours and steam are sucked downwards by an internal fan.

CONTROL KNOBS
Easy-grip, giant knobs make gas burners simple to control.

CERAMIC HALOGEN HOB WITH STEAMER ▽

A ceramic hob flanked by two down-draught extractors, a steamer, and a griddle, packs several distinct cooking functions into a small space. The hardwearing granite worktop surrounding the hob can be used as a "parking" area for hot and heavy pans, and is fireproof.

COVERED GRIDDLE
A hinged lid can be pulled down when not in use to form a "parking" space for pans.

STEAMER WITH LID
If you enjoy steamed foods, this component saves valuable pan space on the hob.

CERAMIC HOB
Fitted with halogen rings, this hob compares favourably in versatility to gas.

HOB EXTRACTOR
Extractors on either side of the hob plate ensure steam and odours are removed.

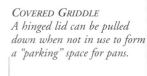

HOBS WITH OVERHEAD EXTRACTION

Condensation can be a problem in many kitchens as pans bubbling away on the hob produce both heat and moisture. To prevent this, and the peeling paint and mould that result, install an extractor. If the extractor has an internal, motorized fan, check that the motor runs quietly when on. If not, see whether the fan can be mounted on an outside wall. If you would rather not have an extractor hood obstructing your headroom, consider a down-draught system (*bottom left*).

▽ **PROFESSIONAL GAS HOB**
Many top-knotch cooks favour gas hobs because they heat up quickly and the temperature is easy to control. Space can be wasted between four burners, but here, the area between pan grids holds two useful pan rests.

LOW-LEVEL HOB ▷
Comparable to gas in flexibility, an induction hob only allows electric energy to be turned into heat inside the cooking pan, so the hob surface remains at a safe, moderate temperature.

PULL-OUT EXTRACTOR
When several pans are on the go, pull out the visor; otherwise tuck it away to maintain clear headroom.

STAINLESS STEEL SIDES
Raised edges improve safety and hygiene, by keeping hot food splashes within the hob area.

PAN STORAGE
Open shelves below the hob are convenient, but grease and dust soon collect on unused pans.

EXTRACTOR HOOD
Ensure task lights are fitted under the hood to light up the hob area.

HOOD HEIGHT
The distance between hood and hob is crucial to the efficiency of the extractor. Take care to follow manufacturer's recommendations.

EXTRACTOR GRILLE
Set against the wall, this system sucks in steam and fumes before they escape into the room.

GAS BURNERS
Unlike electric rings that eventually burn out, gas burners last indefinitely, and the flames are controllable.

HOB HEIGHT

When cooking, you can see inside pans.

Hob sits 10–17.5cm (4–7in) below flexed elbow height.

Place the hob at a lower height than surrounding worktops, to protect the surfaces from fat splashes.

OVEN COOKING

TODAY'S COOK can choose from an extensive range of free-standing and fitted ovens with a choice of cooking options. Some, referred to as "semi-professional", are heavy-duty ovens and resemble those used by restaurant chefs. Beware of being seduced by good looks and list your priorities, such as size, self-cleaning ability, and energy efficiency, before making a decision.

BELOW-DECK OVENS

Many manufacturers produce all-in-one ovens and hobs with either single or double oven facilities. An advantage of combined units is that cooking activities are focused in one part of the kitchen. But if you tend to roast or oven-bake food, you may find bending down to access the oven tiresome. If your kitchen is small, a single oven and hob unit is best but check there is space for the oven door to open.

TRADITIONAL AGA ▷
These enamelled stoves are fired by solid fuels, oil, gas, or electricity, and are constantly hot and ready for use.

FREESTANDING OVEN ▽
A solidly constructed, high-quality appliance such as this features six gas burners, a hot plate and two double ovens. If you cook on a professional basis or have a large family, this oven may be a worthwhile investment.

STAINLESS STEEL SPLASHBACK
A splashback protects kitchen walls from a build-up of grease.

SIMPLE CONTROLS
Easy-grip knobs and pull-down doors make it simple to operate.

STAINLESS STEEL
A durable, brushed stainless steel finish improves with age.

FLAT SIDES
The appliance can be fitted flush to cabinetry if you do not wish it to stand alone.

DOOR VENTILATION
Small vents keep these "child-height" doors cool on the outside.

SEE-THROUGH DOOR
A glass panel helps you check food without opening the door.

STORAGE DRAWER
Baking trays can be neatly stowed away when not in use.

△ **SINGLE OVEN AND HOB**
A compact appliance for those without the space to house a separate oven at eye level. When switched off, the halogen hob doubles up as an extra worktop.

FOUR LEGS
Short legs raise the oven off the ground so that the floor underneath can be swept.

REMEMBER

■ Decide whether an oven at eye level is a priority. Bear in mind that a separate oven and hob, although convenient, may work out more expensive.

■ If you want to fit a powerful, outdoor extractor motor (*see pp.28–29*), ensure the oven and hob sit against an outside wall.

■ Check whether your floor is solid and can take the weight of a heavy stove.

■ If you wish to turn off your Aga during the summer, provide a back-up oven and hob.

EYE-LEVEL OVENS

Easier and safer to load than below-counter ovens, an eye-level appliance has a simple pull-down oven door. The dish is placed inside without the extra effort of bending down, and you can watch your food as it cooks. If you enjoy catering for large numbers of people, a second oven for warming plates, grilling, or microwaving may be advantageous.

OVEN HEIGHT

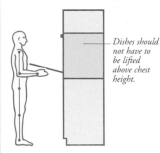

Dishes should not have to be lifted above chest height.

Place a single oven, or two ovens housed in a tall unit, somewhere between eye level and waist height for ease of use.

SLIDE-UP DOOR
One simple action raises the cabinet door that conceals the steamer.

STEAM OVEN
Although costly, consider this type of oven if it suits your eating habits.

SECOND OVEN
For maximum usage, choose a fan-assisted model that can also grill and microwave.

SPACE BELOW
The ovens are fitted at the best height for the user, leaving space for a storage cupboard below.

STEAM OVEN COMBINATION ▷
For those who favour healthy, fat-free cooking techniques, a steam oven is the modern-day pressure cooker. By cooking foods such as fresh vegetables and fish in steam, the moisture is retained. Combine a steam oven with a multi-functional electric oven to cover all options.

◁ DOUBLE OVENS
For keen cooks who enjoy baking, roasting, and grilling, a double oven combined with a separate worktop-mounted hob is perhaps the answer. Opt for a solidly built appliance with easy to interpret controls and fold-down doors that serve as resting platforms for hot dishes entering or leaving the oven.

MICROWAVE AND OVEN ▷
For people with busy schedules, a microwave and electric oven may be the most useful combination. If cooking is really not your priority, install a dishwasher in the cabinet below the microwave instead of an oven, to save on time spent in the kitchen washing-up (*see Family Kitchen Plan pp.70–71*).

EATING

UNLESS YOU HAVE an exceptionally small kitchen, try to include an eating area in your plan because a table is the linchpin for a sociable kitchen. Above all, it is the gathering place where members of the family and friends naturally congregate. For this reason, the table should occupy the most comfortable space in the room, and have at its disposal the best source of natural light, or a window view.

△ AWKWARD-CORNER TABLE
A custom-made triangular table makes imaginative use of an awkward corner. By creating a deep shape, there is enough room for two place settings to fit comfortably without over-cluttering the table-top.

BUILT-IN TABLES

With careful planning, a small table where you can enjoy breakfast or a light supper can usually be accommodated in even the most compact of kitchens. It can also function as an extra work surface or a "parking" space for pans in transit.

TABLE SIZE
The table should have at least 30cm (12in) of space per place setting.

FOLD-UP TABLE AND CHAIRS ▷
A fold-away table can offer an inexpensive solution for those who wish to eat in the kitchen but do not have the space for a permanent fixture. However, these tables can be unstable and make eating cramped.

LAMINATE SURFACE
Ideal for messy children, this table-top is easy to wipe clean but can scratch.

LOW-MAINTENANCE CHAIRS
Choose hard chairs that can be wiped clean rather than upholstered seating.

FOLDING CHAIRS
Lightweight chairs can be folded away when not in use.

BREAKFAST BAR ▽
Wrapped around the cooking zone of an island hob, a granite breakfast bar offers a spacious, horseshoe-shaped table for informal meals.

RAISED BAR HEIGHT
The counter sits above the hob and hides any cooking mess from view.

LEG ROOM
A good fold-up design has space for uninterrupted leg room.

REMEMBER

■ The space allocated for a kitchen table is usually that which is left over once all the other fixtures and fittings have been placed. Try to keep the position of the table in mind when starting your design.

■ The aspect of the table is very important. Consider the best source of natural light and ensure the site is draught-free and warm, especially in winter.

■ Try to plan a cupboard near to the table for storing breakfast materials, table linen, china, glasses, cutlery, and any other table-laying equipment.

■ If you have children, the kitchen table becomes a centre for homework, painting, and other table-top activities. If you opt for a wooden kitchen table, choose one with an oiled rather than lacquered finish as it will be much more hardwearing.

GRANITE TOP
A hardwearing surface that does not burn or stain.

BAR STOOLS
For extra comfort, choose cushioned stools that support the back and have a foot rest.

TABLE SHAPES

For people who do not have a formal dining room, or for those who simply prefer to eat in the relaxed atmosphere of the kitchen, the shape and size of the table is vital. Bear in mind that kitchen tables are usually round, oval, or rectangular, and each shape determines how people interact with one another. Table size is also worth considering because, although the room may be spacious, a large table may not be in keeping with the mood you wish to create, or how often you entertain.

ROUND TABLE ▷

Useful for filling a square kitchen floor area, small, round tables offer an intimate setting for four people, and are democratic as no one sits at the head. Large, round tables are less successful because of their wide diameter, which leaves guests raising their voices to be heard.

FOUR-SEATER TABLE
A table just over 1m (3ft 3in) in diameter seats four comfortably.

ELBOW ROOM

Each place setting is 30cm (12in) deep.

Allow a 55cm (22in) width of table space per person for eating without restriction, plus an extra 5cm (2in) on either side of each place, for chair movement without disruption.

OVAL TABLE ▽

An oval is perhaps the most successful shape for seating six people, as everyone can make eye contact. The generous centre space stops the table-top from becoming over crowded.

INSET LEG
Slim legs allow space for two chairs at each end, to seat eight.

SEATING
If you want to save space taken up by separate chairs, build a banquette along one wall.

TABLE SIZE
This oval is 1.6m (5ft 3in) long x 1.3m (4ft 3in) wide at the centre.

RECTANGULAR TABLE ▽

For those who have a large family or who love to entertain, choose a large, rectangular table that seats up to ten people. Here, eating is a communal activity, but of course a dining table of this scale needs a large kitchen.

LONG TABLE
At least 2m (6ft 6in) long, the huge distance between ends can divide guests into two groups.

WASHING-UP

THE WASHING-UP AREA is used more intensively than any other activity zone in the kitchen, so apply careful thought to its arrangement. There are several ergonomic aspects to resolve: the height of the sink; the depth of the washing bowl; the amount of space given over to draining; the proximity of china and cutlery storage; and the position of the sink cabinet to ensure an interesting viewpoint.

REMEMBER

■ Try to keep the distance between the sink, hob, and worktop areas to a minimum as food preparation and cooking involves constant rinsing and cleaning of used utensils.

■ Consider the variety of tasks you wish to perform at the sink before deciding whether one large sink bowl or two or three smaller bowls would best suit your needs. Is the sink to be used solely for pans and oven trays, or for hand-washing crockery and glasses as well?

■ Arrange the sink cabinet so that there is enough space for draining boards on either side, and so that it has a pleasant aspect, perhaps a garden view.

■ If you intend to have a dishwasher, consider installing the appliance at a raised height, to avoid constant stooping down to load the machine.

WASHING-UP BY HAND

Tailor your sink to your washing needs. If you cater for a large family on a regular basis, opt for a heavy-duty sink with long draining boards that is large enough for soaking big pots, oven pans, and chopping boards. A more compact unit will suit those who wash up one or two light meals a day.

TALL TOP SHELF
Although difficult to reach, less regularly used items can be kept here.

CROCKERY STORAGE
Glass-fronted cupboards and a plate rack provide storage within arm's reach.

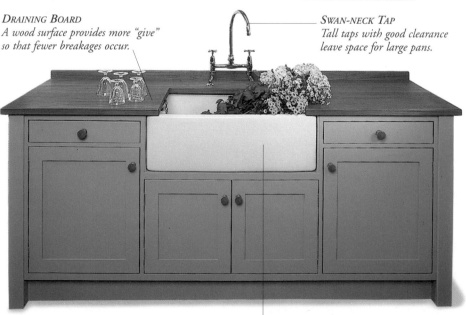

DRAINING BOARD
A wood surface provides more "give" so that fewer breakages occur.

SWAN-NECK TAP
Tall taps with good clearance leave space for large pans.

SINK HEIGHT

Avoid deep basins, as they will put extra strain on your back.

The ideal height for the top of the sink is 5cm (2in) below the base of a flexed elbow. The sink cabinet may sit slightly above waist height but there will be no need to lean over the basin.

BELFAST SINK △
This old-fashioned design has the advantage of being wide, deep, and also robust. It is installed without a frame, which means that the porcelain is visible and there is only a short distance to reach over into the sink. For it to function as a double sink for rinsing and washing, place a small plastic bowl inside the porcelain one.

WHITE PORCELAIN
Porcelain-coated fire clay offers a stain- and heat-resistant surface.

ANGLED WASHING-UP UNIT ▷
In a small kitchen, a wedge-shaped unit with a compact draining area contains this kitchen activity while freeing up space for a greater expanse of worktop.

DOWNLIGHTERS
Built-in task lights above the sink provide a strong light and prevent a shadow being cast over this small area as you work.

COVERED RACK
Plates and cups drain directly into the sink and then, when dry, remain neatly stored behind a hinged door.

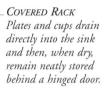

CLEANING AGENTS
These are stowed on racks at eye level to keep the sink area uncluttered.

STAINLESS STEEL
Raised sides and a wide overhang prevent water overflowing onto the cabinet and floor below.

CURVED EDGE
For safety and good looks, the cabinet has a curved side rather than a sharp, angular edge.

DISHWASHERS

Research a number of products and compare reliability and life expectancy of the machines. Choose a model with valuable features, such as high energy efficiency, low operating noise levels, two revolving spray arms for a thorough wash, anti-flood sensors, removable racks, and variable-sized plate and glass holders. Bear in mind that smaller, slimline models are available.

▽ **COMBINED APPLIANCE**
Small kitchens quickly become chaotic if dishes are left to pile up unwashed on worktops. Make use of your sink plumbing to install a dishwasher underneath your sink unit at little extra cost.

GRANITE SURFACE
A hardwearing granite worktop provides a stain-resistant surface.

INSIDE THE MACHINE
Stainless steel interiors are more durable and less likely to stain and take on odours.

DOOR CLEARANCE
If the kitchen is narrow, make sure there is ample space to walk around the door when it is open.

HARDWARE STORAGE

USER-FRIENDLY CROCKERY, glass, and kitchen equipment storage relies on clever organization, so that items taken out frequently are stored within reach – somewhere between knee height and eye level – and close to the activity area where they are needed. Much of this kitchenware is brought out, washed, and put back several times a day, so proximity to the sink or dishwasher also saves trips across the kitchen.

HIDDEN STORAGE

Kitchen hardware left out in the room on display and not used on a day-to-day basis soon gathers dust or becomes coated in a layer of grease. To avoid extra cleaning, or for those who prefer to keep worktops free of clutter, place items behind closed doors. Order the internal space so that frequently used equipment is near the front, and try to avoid storage systems with deep shelves.

LARGE BOWLS ON DISPLAY
Kitchen pieces add charm, but take them down regularly to clean.

SHELF DEPTH

Store items used daily between knee height and eye level.

To avoid having to stretch, the ideal depth of shelving should not exceed 60cm (24in) to the back of the cupboard. Any deeper would be hard to reach.

COURT CUPBOARD ▷
A 19th-century Irish food cupboard with four doors and two drawers offers both an attractive and practical storage facility. A large cupboard placed against a kitchen wall has a greater storage capacity than does a row of fitted base units and wall units in the same space.

CUPBOARD HEIGHT
The top shelf is within arm's reach, as the full height of the cupboard is only 1.9m (6ft 2in).

UTENSIL DRAWER
Store utensils in compartments to keep them sharp and in good condition.

△ UTENSILS BELOW HOB
A shallow drawer, running below the hob, is divided up into nine front and nine back sections to keep smaller utensils in order. Each compartment has a curved base so that you can scoop out a utensil as it is required.

PAN DRAWER
A laminate finish ensures a hardwearing interior.

△ STORING PANS
Like other kitchen hardware, pans should be stored close to the activity area. If you prefer your pans to be put away, one option is to install a deep drawer, below the hob, on strong runners that are fully extendable.

REMEMBER

■ Ask yourself whether the storage system you favour actually suits your needs. If you do not think your collection of hardware is attractive enough to display, choose closed units.

■ Make sure that the shelf system you select has adjustable shelf heights to suit both large and small pieces of crockery, glassware, small electrical appliances, and pans.

VISIBLE STORAGE

All kitchens gain in atmosphere when pots and pans, and other items associated with cooking and eating food, are on view. The most successful open storage systems, whether traditional or contemporary, are those where a sense of order prevails, and practical and aesthetic considerations are well-balanced. For example, plates placed upright (*below*) not only look good but collect less dust on their surface.

CARVED CUPBOARD
Traditional features make the kitchen feel well-furnished, like other rooms.

DOOR WIDTH
Approximately 60cm (24in) wide, the doors are not too obtrusive when open.

DRAWER SPACE
House cutlery, table mats, instruction leaflets, and cut-out recipes in these generous drawers.

DUST-FREE STORAGE
Crockery kept behind closed doors is less susceptible to dust and grease-laden kitchen fumes.

INDIVIDUAL COMPARTMENTS
A separate display space allocated to each item enhances the sense of order.

SAUCEPAN TREE ▷
If an awkward corner exists close to your hob, a pan stand may be a useful storage feature, although take care, as tall stands can be slightly unstable.

PAN SIZE
Store progressively larger and heavier pans on lower levels.

◁ **TRADITIONAL DRESSER**
An antique dresser with its open shelves, hooks, drawers, and cupboards, provides a decorative but practical way to store and display cups, plates, cutlery, and glasses.

CUP HOOKS
Hang cups on the front edge of the shelves so that they do not take up valuable shelf space.

CUPBOARD SPACE
Store less decorative, utilitarian items on shelves behind doors.

▽ **OPEN-FRONTED AND GLASS UNIT**
A built-in full-height system for those who like to be able to display decorative crockery and store utilitarian items in the same unit. Fit the unit on a wall linking cooking and eating areas.

PULL-OUT DRAWER
Semi-translucent glass removes the tyranny of maintaining a neat display.

SLIDING GLASS DOOR
A good compromise, for even when the door is shut you can quickly locate items.

WORKTOPS

IN WELL-DESIGNED kitchens, individual countertops are built from different materials that change from one activity zone to the next. The choice of material is lead by the task undertaken as there is no one surface that can withstand scratches, stains and heat marks, and be hardwearing, easy to clean, and attractive. Compare the merits of each surface before choosing.

POINTS TO CONSIDER

■ Cover the area surrounding the hob with terrazzo, granite, or stainless steel. All three are heatproof, hardwearing, and require little effort to maintain. If you are not planning to stay in your property for long, the cost of these materials may be a drawback.

■ For draining boards, the most appropriate materials are water-resistant, and provide a soft landing for delicate china and glassware that have to be washed by hand. Stainless steel, oiled hardwood, Colorcore, and Corian are all suitable materials.

■ Chopping and food preparation is best performed on wood. Consider buying a series of different-sized blocks to lay on top of any surface, or install a slab of end-grain wood. Once regarded as a breeding ground for bacteria, wood is now known to be hygienic.

■ Granite or slate are both suitable surfaces for pastry-making because they are cool and smooth, so preventing pastry from sticking.

■ Oiled hardwoods make attractive and easy to restore general surfaces, when away from heat.

STAINLESS STEEL

A near-perfect worktop material, used in professional kitchens where performance is important. A brushed finish is best.

ADVANTAGES
• A non-corrosive and heatproof material.
• Wipes clean easily and is very hygienic.
• Brushed stainless steel wears particularly well.

DISADVANTAGES
• Highly polished surfaces scratch easily.
• A noisy surface to work on.
• Difficult to fabricate into curved shapes.

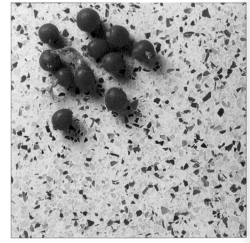

GRANITE

A natural material available in a huge range of colours and patterns. It is cut to size and polished to make worktops.

ADVANTAGES
• Natural beauty does not deteriorate with age.
• Almost impossible to scratch or chip.
• Heatproof, waterproof, and difficult to stain.

DISADVANTAGES
• Expensive as it is a hard stone to machine-cut.
• Weight requires base cabinets to be strong.
• Dark colourways can appear cold and murky.

SLATE

Many slates are too porous for kitchen use but a few newly available types have a high silica content that reduces porosity.

ADVANTAGES
• Smooth surface is cool and pleasant to touch.
• Relatively hardwearing if silica content is high.
• A cheaper alternative to granite and marble.

DISADVANTAGES
• Porous types of slate absorb oil and stain easily.
• A finish must be applied to reduce porosity.
• Colours can be dull and uninteresting.

TERRAZZO

A lesser known material, made from a mixture of marble and granite chippings set in white cement, and then polished.

ADVANTAGES
• Comes in wide variety of colours and patterns.
• Can be made up to your exact specification.
• Hardwearing and waterproof.

DISADVANTAGES
• Costly and time-consuming to install.
• Not as hardwearing as natural stones.
• Bolder patterns may lose their appeal in time.

LACQUERED HARDWOOD

The beauty of wood makes it a popular choice. These worktops are coated with lacquer, above and below, for protection.

ADVANTAGES
• Wide range of different colours and grains exist.
• Worktops match the wood cabinet finishes.
• Reasonably priced.

DISADVANTAGES
• Liquid spillages eventually dissolve the lacquer.
• Knife cuts permanently damage the surface.
• Not as hardwearing as other wood finishes.

END-GRAIN WOOD

As its name suggests, this is wood turned on its end and glued together in blocks. It provides the best surface for cutting.

ADVANTAGES
• Very dense and wears evenly across the grain.
• Knife blades do not damage the end-grain.
• Blade is gripped on contact, making it safer.

DISADVANTAGES
• Central heating may cause the worktop to warp.
• Absorbs strong food flavours, such as garlic.
• Wood may contract in centrally heated homes.

OILED WOOD

Planks of solid hardwood that are glued together and brushed with linseed oil to prevent the wood from splitting.

ADVANTAGES
• More resistant to heat than lacquered wood.
• Flexible surface that can withstand knocks.
• Sanding and a coat of oil restores its beauty.

DISADVANTAGES
• Central heating may cause it to warp or crack.
• Chopping on this surface leaves deep incisions.
• Some oiled hardwoods are expensive.

FORMICA LAMINATE

A man-made material that has a paper centre and is built up with thick coats of lacquer to create a flexible sheet material.

ADVANTAGES
• Huge choice of bright colours and patterns.
• Waterproof and easy to wipe clean.
• Simple and inexpensive to manufacture.

DISADVANTAGES
• Cutting directly onto the surface causes damage.
• In time, the laminate can deteriorate.
• Once damaged, the worktop cannot be repaired.

COLORCORE

This material is made from layer upon layer of coloured paper, coated in a tough melamine-formaldehyde resin.

ADVANTAGES
• Knife cuts on worktops can be sanded away.
• Subtle range of colours is available.
• Waterproof and simple to wipe clean.

DISADVANTAGES
• More expensive than Formica laminate.
• Can become unstuck at the edges.
• Surface has no light-reflective qualities.

CORIAN

A synthetic resin best installed in heavily used areas, such as around sinks, where it can be seamlessly joined to worktops.

ADVANTAGES
• Rounded front edges are safer for small children.
• Joins between different sections are invisible.
• Sinks and worktops are made from one piece.

DISADVANTAGES
• Difficult to install without professional help.
• Over long periods, paler colours may yellow.
• Can work out as expensive as granite.

CABINET FINISHES

WHEN YOU HAVE DECIDED what cabinetry you would like in your new kitchen, consider the finish. Although this may seem a minor decorative detail, the choice of materials presents a major opportunity to influence the atmosphere of the room. Bear in mind that different surface finishes affect the quality of light. High-gloss or shiny finishes increase reflections and glare, while matt finishes are kinder on the eyes and diffuse light. Pale-coloured units will brighten up dark kitchens, as will glass cabinets, while dark wood and dark synthetic finishes absorb light.

GLASS

Glass wall-cabinets are useful in small kitchens where they open up the space, and display decorative kitchen items.

ADVANTAGES
• Surface is easy to wipe clean with a soft cloth.
• Stored items are visible so are easy to find.
• Light-reflective quality brightens up dark rooms.

DISADVANTAGES
• Smudges of grease and dirt show on glass.
• Only neat, attractive items can be stored.
• Susceptible to knocks and may crack.

COMBINATION OF FINISHES
This adventurous design contrasts cherry wood with deep blue sprayed lacquer.

STAINLESS STEEL

Offering a durable metal finish that does not tarnish or rust, this surface works well near sinks and cooking areas.

ADVANTAGES
• Attractive surface sheen reflects light.
• Contrasts well with wood and painted surfaces.
• Matches appliances finished in stainless steel.

DISADVANTAGES
• Fingermarks and watermarks show up easily.
• Easy to scratch, especially polished finishes.
• Too much stainless steel looks clinical.

POINTS TO CONSIDER

■ When you have finalized your room plan, choose the finish for the cabinets at the same time as flooring, wallcoverings, lighting, and worktops – the interior design scheme.

■ The balance of colours and finishes is important. Too much of any one finish is overpowering and some, such as high-gloss polyester and brightly coloured lacquers, are particularly overwhelming. These should be used only in small quantities, offset by natural materials like wood.

■ Ask yourself whether the kitchen design can be enhanced by using a combination of cabinet finishes to distinguish the key activity areas in the room.

■ List your favourite finishes in order of preference. Calculate how much each finish will cost to see what is affordable within your budget. Limiting expensive finishes to a few key areas and combining them with other materials will help to keep costs down.

■ Select hardwearing materials for cabinets in intensively used areas and, if kitchen traffic is heavy or you have children, select the most durable finishes for base units.

■ If you cannot afford to fit new kitchen cabinets, give the existing units a facelift simply by replacing or painting the cabinet doors and changing the style of handles to suit your taste.

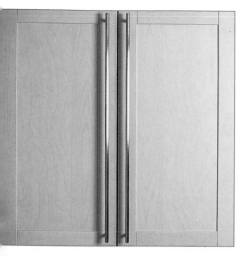

WOOD VENEER

High-quality woods are often sliced into veneers, so for those who favour a wood kitchen, veneers can offer the best finish.

ADVANTAGES
• Colour and texture are easy to live with.
• Grain configuration is better than solid wood.
• Unlike solid wood finishes, veneer does not warp.

DISADVANTAGES
• If moisture seeps in, the veneer may peel.
• Uniform tone and colour may be monotonous.
• High-quality veneers can be expensive.

HAND-PAINTED WOOD

In contrast to smooth, synthetic finishes, these cabinets are painted by hand and can be "distressed" to add extra character.

ADVANTAGES
• Can select precise colour to match your scheme.
• Damaged units can be repaired by repainting.
• Variability of finish between units adds charm.

DISADVANTAGES
• Needs several coats of varnish to protect it.
• Not as durable as other cabinet finishes.
• May need repainting in time.

CHICKEN WIRE

An unusual cabinet finish that appears purely decorative; however, stored items are kept well-ventilated and dust-free.

ADVANTAGES
• Chicken wire enables air to circulate inside.
• Decorative effect with "country style" appeal.
• Inexpensive; easy to build without expert help.

DISADVANTAGES
• Dust may gather on fabric, making it unhygienic.
• Appearance limits it to one style of kitchen.
• Chicken wire can stretch and distort.

POLYESTER

Offered by only a few manufacturers, this synthetic resin is sprayed thickly onto the cabinet for a high-gloss finish.

ADVANTAGES
• Smooth, high-gloss finishes are available.
• Hardwearing finish is easy to wipe clean.
• Available in a huge range of bold colours.

DISADVANTAGES
• Glossy surface shows up greasy fingermarks.
• More expensive than other synthetic finishes.
• High-gloss finish may cause kitchen glare.

LAMINATE

An economical plastic sheet material made from melamine, which is then glued onto a cabinet panel.

ADVANTAGES
• Both colour and pattern are unlimited.
• More economical than other synthetic finishes.
• Can withstand knocks.

DISADVANTAGES
• If scratched, the finish cannot be repaired.
• Reflects light poorly and looks artificial.
• Laminates can lift at the corners if damp.

SPRAYED LACQUER

A clear lacquer is spray-painted onto the outside of a stained or painted cabinet to provide a protective finish.

ADVANTAGES
• Hardwearing protective finish.
• Easy to wipe clean.
• Less expensive than a polyester finish.

DISADVANTAGES
• Impossible to repair on site.
• Finish can look flat and lack-lustre.
• More expensive than a laminate finish.

WALLCOVERINGS

SELECTING A WALL finish for your new kitchen is not simply a style issue. The kitchen is often the most-used room in the home, and hot and steamy conditions put special demands even on the walls. The wall areas that take the most abuse are those behind the sink cabinet, hob and oven, and food preparation worktops. Stray splashes soon spoil wallpaper or paint, so install a guard made from an easy-wipe material. It is details such as these that will help you create not just a kitchen with character but one that is a pleasure to work in.

PROTECTIVE WALL FINISH
The cooking range sits in an alcove that has been tiled to provide an easy-clean surface.

POINTS TO CONSIDER

■ When you have chosen countertops and cabinetry, think about the walls. Consider wallcoverings that either match or contrast with the cabinet finishes. Pay particular attention to the wall area between the worktop and the wall cupboard, known as the splashback.

■ Try choosing a splashback that contrasts with the dominant material. For example, natural wood cabinetry looks good with a dark granite splashback.

■ For the splashback behind the hob, choose a heat-resistant material, such as stainless steel, ceramic tile, or natural stone.

■ If you decide to paint the walls, choose oil-based or gloss paint finishes that are durable and can be washed down. Avoid emulsion paints, especially if ventilation is poor, because they do not stand up so well to condensation.

■ If the kitchen has a high percentage of plastic finishes, use natural materials, such as wood panelling, to redress the balance.

■ If the room is north-facing or has a low ceiling, use paler colours on the walls to reflect light from windows, and to create a feeling of space. A splashback of etched glass will also help to reflect light onto worktops.

PLASTER WALLS

Once a technique for preparing walls, bare plaster is now a popular wall finish and comes rough, polished, or stained.

ADVANTAGES
• Masks uneven walls, turning them into a feature.
• Durable and inexpensive finish.
• Provides an opportunity to add character.

DISADVANTAGES
• Rough plaster attracts dust and is hard to clean.
• Can look artificial if not well rendered.
• Requires a splashback around countertops.

DECORATIVE GLASS

Rarely used in kitchens, the waterproof and heat-resistant properties of glass make it a good choice for splashbacks.

ADVANTAGES
• Useful around sink areas and cooking zones.
• Easy to wipe clean.
• Reflects light, and introduces a decorative finish.

DISADVANTAGES
• Difficult to transport to site and install.
• May break if struck with a hard object.
• Expensive as specially cut from templates to fit.

OIL-BASED PAINT

The most versatile kitchen wallcovering of all, select paints with hardwearing oil-based finishes, such as eggshell and gloss.

ADVANTAGES
• Wide range of colours with durable finishes.
• Walls can be wiped clean with a sponge.
• Simple to retouch small areas or repaint room.

DISADVANTAGES
• Not tough enough to be used as a splashback.
• Gloss paints show up imperfections in walls.
• Painted walls may peel or become mildewed.

WASHABLE WALLPAPER

Plastic-coated, wipe-clean wallpapers are practical, especially if you have very small children, but colour choice is limited.

ADVANTAGES
• Waterproof plastic surface is easy to wipe clean.
• Can be put up after cabinetry is installed.
• Inexpensive; covers up uneven plasterwork.

DISADVANTAGES
• Steam may cause wallpaper to peel.
• Plastic "sheen" on surface can look artificial.
• Impossible to repair small area once damaged.

WOOD PANELLING

Useful for covering up uneven areas on walls and ceilings, painted wood panels will also help insulate heat and sound.

ADVANTAGES
• Easy to install without expert help.
• Hides irregular walls or uneven plasterwork.
• Absorbs kitchen noise.

DISADVANTAGES
• Good quality panelling not always available.
• Unsuitable material for sink and cooking area.
• Traditional look does not suit all kitchen styles.

MANUFACTURED TILES

Less expensive than handmade tiles, these are ideal for tiling large expanses of wall, perhaps behind a hob or sink.

ADVANTAGES
• Easy-to-clean flat surface and thin grouting.
• Heat-resistant, so suitable for cooking areas.
• Pale tiles covering large areas look inoffensive.

DISADVANTAGES
• Regular shape and surface can look boring.
• Can detract from character of room.
• Darker coloured tiles can be less hardwearing.

HANDMADE TILES

Available in a vivid range of colours and finishes, these hardwearing tiles offer great decorative possibilities in kitchens.

ADVANTAGES
• Handmade quality adds character to kitchen.
• Wide range of colours, finishes, and sizes.
• Hardwearing and waterproof.

DISADVANTAGES
• Uneven shape tiles require thicker grouting.
• Grouting collects dirt and takes time to clean.
• Patterned tiles can become difficult to live with.

GRANITE

This popular kitchen material is often used as a splashback above granite worktops. It works best in small areas.

ADVANTAGES
• Hardwearing and low-maintenance.
• Easy to clean, with few grouted seams.
• Continuity; it can match a granite worktop.

DISADVANTAGES
• Dark, cold appearance unsuitable for large areas.
• Complicated to fit around plug sockets.
• Expensive; has to be cut off-site, to a template.

FLOORINGS

CHOOSING THE RIGHT material for your new kitchen floor needs careful thought. It is a delicate balancing act between finding a hardwearing, hygienic material, aesthetic preferences, and budget. Wooden floors are warm, easy to sweep clean, and good value but long-term durability and water-resistance around the sink unit are a problem; limestone and slate are hardwearing but can be cold and hard on the feet. Modern materials, such as vinyl, are also appealing because, although they are not as long-lasting as natural materials, they are lower in cost and easier to replace when worn.

WOOD

The warmth of colour, choice of grains, and "give" underfoot make natural wood popular, but it must be well-sealed.

ADVANTAGES
- Reasonably priced and straightforward to install.
- China often "bounces" when dropped on wood.
- It complements wood cabinetry and worktops.

DISADVANTAGES
- Few protective finishes last, especially when wet.
- Too much wood in one room is overpowering.
- Requires regular maintenance.

VARNISHED WOOD FLOORING
A strip-pine floor is good value, and complements the simplicity of this painted wood kitchen.

LIMESTONE TILES

Enthusiasm for this natural stone means that quarried limestone is easy to obtain. Choose one with a low level of porosity.

ADVANTAGES
- A wide choice of colours, textures, and patterns.
- Durable and low maintenance if properly sealed.
- Resistant to heat, water, and household solvents.

DISADVANTAGES
- Some porous types need several coats of sealant.
- Hard surface is cold on the feet and noisy.
- Lighter colours show up dirt easily.

POINTS TO CONSIDER

■ Think carefully about your selection of materials for cabinet finishes, countertops, appliances, and soft furnishings before making a final decision on flooring. This way you can ensure that all the elements in the kitchen complement one another. Do not forget to look at the floor in the hall or adjacent rooms; too many changes of finish from one room to the next in a small house can appear fussy and tiresome.

■ Bear in mind the cost of laying the floor as well as the purchase price of materials. All floors, except vinyl and linoleum, should be layed before cabinetry and appliances are installed. Ensure the new floor is well protected during other installations.

■ The amount of day-to-day maintenance you are willing to undertake may influence your floor choice. Some materials, such as wood, require more care, especially around the sink, where water damages the varnish.

■ Decide whether the kitchen is large enough to accommodate two floor finishes. You may prefer limestone tiles around the cooking zone where activity is concentrated, and wood flooring in the eating area.

■ If you choose tiled flooring, bear in mind that large rooms need large, plain tiles; small, patterned tiles will look too busy. Flagstones and large terracotta tiles suit the proportions of huge family kitchens.

GLAZED CERAMIC TILES

The most hardwearing and impermeable of all flooring materials. Glazed ceramic tiles do not need sealing for protection.

ADVANTAGES
• Low maintenance and almost indestructible.
• Mass-produced, so easy and inexpensive to buy.
• Available in a huge range of bold colours.

DISADVANTAGES
• Hard on feet and slippery when wet.
• Grout between tiles can be difficult to clean.
• Strong-coloured glazes can be overpowering.

TERRACOTTA TILES

Brand new and reclaimed terracotta tiles are available. In time, new tiles develop the rich patina common to old ones.

ADVANTAGES
• Clay is warmer than stone underfoot.
• Variety of colours, textures, shapes, and sizes.
• Sealed tiles are water- and stain-resistant.

DISADVANTAGES
• Unsealed tiles are porous and stain easily.
• Difficult to find matching old tiles in quantity.
• High-quality tiles can be expensive.

SLATE

Popular because of its natural variations in colour from grey to green and purple, slate is precision-cut into sheets or tiles.

ADVANTAGES
• Wide range of colours and sizes of slate available.
• Choice of smooth or rough natural finishes.
• Wears well over the years and is waterproof.

DISADVANTAGES
• Large pieces are brittle and may crack or peel.
• Hard and cold underfoot.
• Large sheets of slate are expensive.

CORK TILES

Manufactured by compressing cork, this flooring is inexpensive but rather dull in comparison to other natural floorings.

ADVANTAGES
• Warm and soft underfoot, and extremely quiet.
• Inexpensive and easy to lay without expert help.
• Sealed cork tiles are stain-resistant.

DISADVANTAGES
• Colour, texture, and pattern is uniform and dull.
• Tiles are only stuck down with glue so may lift.
• Tiles damaged by water will need replacing.

VINYL

A cheap, flexible plastic that is produced in sheet or tile form. It is available in a huge range of colours and patterns.

ADVANTAGES
• Soft and quiet underfoot, and non-slip.
• Inexpensive and easy to lay on a flat surface.
• Hardwearing and waterproof.

DISADVANTAGES
• Tends to discolour with age.
• Reflects light poorly and looks artificial.
• Ripples may form if laid on an uneven floor.

LINOLEUM

Produced from natural ingredients, such as linseed oil, linoleum comes in sheets or is hand-cut for intricate patterning.

ADVANTAGES
• A quiet, warm surface that cushions your feet.
• Manufactured from all-natural substances.
• Durable and low-maintenance.

DISADVANTAGES
• More costly than vinyl and needs expert fitting.
• Water can seep under unsealed edges.
• It may scuff or mark if not kept well-polished.

LIGHTING

A WELL-DESIGNED lighting system is a vital ingredient for achieving a pleasant working and eating environment in the kitchen. As electrical fittings have to be installed well before cabinetry and appliances, decide at an early stage in your kitchen design where in the room directional task lights or softer ambient lighting are needed. The exact position of the fittings is also important; if installed too far back from the wall units, you will always be standing in front of the light source and casting a shadow over your work.

TASK LIGHT

CEILING DOWNLIGHTS

Low-voltage downlighters are discreet. Place them 1m (3ft 3in) apart, and 30cm (12in) from the wall to avoid shadows.

ADVANTAGES
• Strong, directional light spotlights worktop area.
• Recessed fitting is protected and free from dust.
• Reduced glare when viewed from a distance.

DISADVANTAGES
• Wall-mounted units can block the light cast.
• The angle of the light can be difficult to adjust.
• Bulbs in some fittings can be hard to remove.

MULTI-PURPOSE LIGHTING SYSTEM
Track lights link kitchen and eating areas; undercabinet lights illuminate the worktops.

ATMOSPHERIC LIGHT

STANDARD UPLIGHT

Designed for eating or relaxation areas in larger kitchens, this freestanding light is operated on a dimmer switch.

ADVANTAGES
• Flexible; it can be moved around where needed.
• Boosts light in dark, forgotten corners.
• Light never shines directly into your eyes.

DISADVANTAGES
• Needs to be positioned near a wall socket.
• Unsuitable for small areas as takes up floor space.
• Away from the source, the light is cold and weak.

POINTS TO CONSIDER

■ Low-voltage lights have two main advantages. They use 30 per cent less electricity than ordinary bulbs and are much smaller, but they do require a transformer to make them compatible with the mains voltage. Some low-voltage lights have built-in transformers but others have a separate element that needs to be hidden. Consult an expert.

■ Check what material your kitchen ceiling is made from because you will not be able to fit recessed downlighters into concrete. To solve this you will need to build a false lower ceiling out of plasterboard. Ask a specialist if you are unsure.

■ You will need to plan a minimum of two electrical circuits for a small kitchen, one for task lights and one for general lighting, and up to five circuits for a large room: one to two circuits for worktops, the front of cabinets, and the table; one uplighter circuit for the ceiling; and one circuit to light a sitting area, plus an extra booster circuit to light lesser areas.

■ Ask an electrician to check whether your fusebox can cope with your lighting needs, whether the circuits are shared with other rooms, and whether the lights can be routed to work with other electrical appliances. Ask for an estimate to help plan your budget.

UNDERCUPBOARD LIGHT

Used to light shadowy areas under wall-mounted units, a fluorescent tube is hidden behind a length of cabinet trim.

ADVANTAGES
• Lights up potentially dark areas on worktops.
• Cheaper to install than halogen downlighters.
• Solves the problem of working in your shadow.

DISADVANTAGES
• Fluorescent tubes cast a harsh, clinical light.
• In time, fluorescent tubes may start to "hum".
• Brightness focuses attention on the worktops.

TRACK SPOTLIGHTS

Wall- and ceiling-mounted tracks offer flexible lighting, but the lamps become hot and must be out of a child's reach.

ADVANTAGES
• Tracks are low-cost and easy to install.
• Flexible; as lamps are multi-directional.
• Task lights can be placed on walls and ceilings.

DISADVANTAGES
• Generate considerable heat and burn if touched.
• Exposed lamps collect dust and are hard to clean.
• Can cause eye-burn if stared at for too long.

CLIP SPOTLIGHT

A temporary solution for unexpected lighting demands, the light cast is limited and cables can get in the way.

ADVANTAGES
• Inexpensive to buy and no installation costs.
• Task light directed exactly where you want it.
• Simple fittings are often well-designed.

DISADVANTAGES
• Cables can obstruct other kitchen activities.
• Uses sockets needed for electrical appliances.
• Needs to be clipped onto a suitable feature.

WALL UPLIGHTS

Suitable for high-ceilinged rooms, they cast an atmospheric light when placed 30–60cm (12–24in) from the ceiling.

ADVANTAGES
• Cheap to install if have same voltage as mains.
• Fills wall space in "low-demand" area near ceiling.
• Creates a different mood for kitchen eating.

DISADVANTAGES
• Only works as a secondary light source.
• Inappropriate for rooms with low ceilings.
• May need a high-wattage lamp on a dimmer.

PENDANT TABLE LIGHT

Hanging above the kitchen table, a pendant light creates a separate lighting environment for informal dining.

ADVANTAGES
• Creates a strong identity for the table area.
• All other lights can be switched off when eating.
• Lowers the ceiling to create an intimate space.

DISADVANTAGES
• Table position in kitchen has to stay fixed.
• People may hit their heads as they sit down.
• Works best with round or square-shaped tables.

CANDLE-LIGHT

If you do not have a dining room, use candles to transform a meal in the kitchen into a special occasion.

ADVANTAGES
• Softens a harsh kitchen environment.
• Makes dining in the kitchen an event.
• Disguises half-tidy worktops and cooking areas.

DISADVANTAGES
• Trips to the stove mid-meal can be difficult.
• Several candles are needed to see food properly.
• Smoke from candles may trigger a smoke alarm.

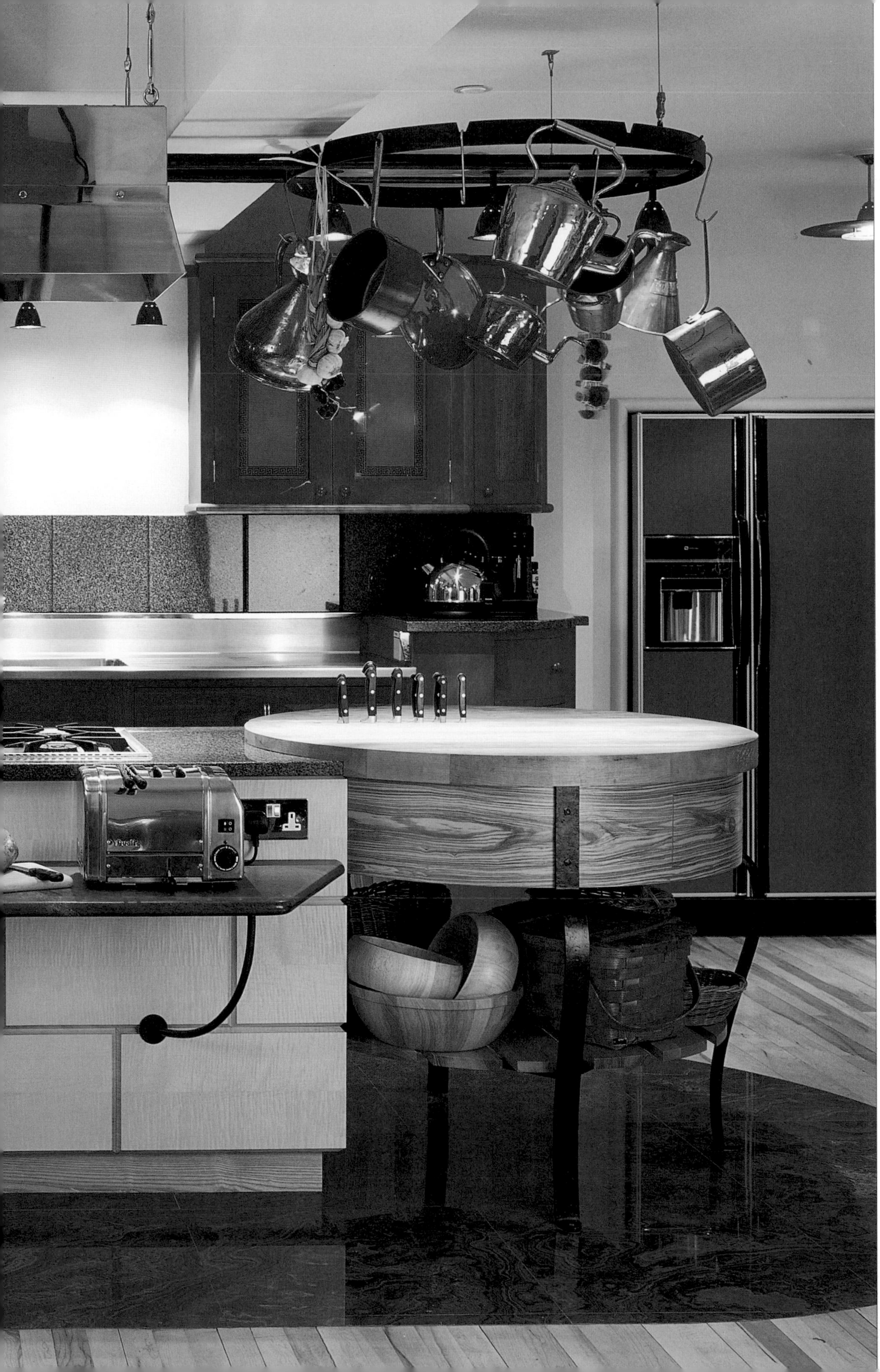

ROOM PLANS

SMALL KITCHEN PLAN

IN A SMALL ROOM, focus on your primary kitchen needs, mapping out the area for the cooker, the sink, and food preparation. Establish the minimum dimensions you can work within without feeling cramped, and then arrange other appliances and storage around this core. Capitalize on every available space from floor to ceiling, and select durable finishes that can adapt to a variety of uses.

TALL APPLIANCE STACK
Solid floor to ceiling units are placed around a corner to minimize their impact.

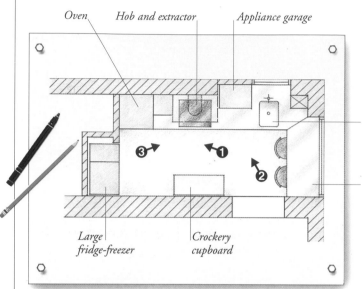

Oven   Hob and extractor   Appliance garage

INTERNAL ROOM
DIMENSIONS:
1.9m (6ft 2in) WIDE
4.4m (14ft 4in) LONG

Single sink

Bar eating area

Large fridge-freezer   Crockery cupboard

△ BIRD'S EYE VIEW
The sink and eating areas benefit from the best natural light and window views, and the hob is against an outside wall to ensure good ventilation. Other kitchen appliances sit behind cabinetry so as not to obstruct the flow of traffic.

FRIDGE-FREEZER
A full-height fridge-freezer is concealed behind cabinetry to make it less obtrusive.

LARDER CUPBOARD
A pull-out larder sits next to the fridge; fresh and dried produce can be picked up in one trip.

DESIGN POINTS

■ In a small space, the close proximity of tasks is inevitable, but check that you can move about the room freely.

■ Install eye-level appliances in tall cabinets at one end of the room and try to leave the rest open to create a feeling of space in a small room.

■ Check that worktops can double up for other activities. In this kitchen, the eating bar is also used for food preparation.

■ Some appliances have reverse hinging – doors opening in the opposite direction may solve a few of your space problems.

STORAGE CUPBOARD
Storage facilities are designed to fit in above and below major appliances.

EYE-LEVEL OVEN
Hot dishes from the tall oven unit can be set down quickly on the worktop to the right.

GLASS-FRONTED UNIT
Crockery and glassware are stored on view within reach of the dishwasher.

◁ ❶ OPENING UP THE SPACE
The halogen hob sits flush against the worktop, and can serve as a preparation area when not in use. A single cupboard, a slender extractor, and task lights keep this area bright and open.

TRACTOR
-limline extractor removes food
ours and steam, which can be
roblem in small kitchens.

❷ DURABLE FINISHES ▷

Stainless steel is used on every horizontal surface because it is heat- and water-resistant, while the cabinets below have a tough melamine finish to protect them from knocks in a tight workplace.

APPLIANCE GARAGE
This utilizes the full depth of the worktop; an appliance can be stored at the back and pulled out onto the worksurface when needed.

WINDOW VIEW
The sink has a view to make washing-up a more enjoyable task.

EYE-LEVEL
MICROWAVE
The oven is placed at an accessible height, leaving the countertop free.

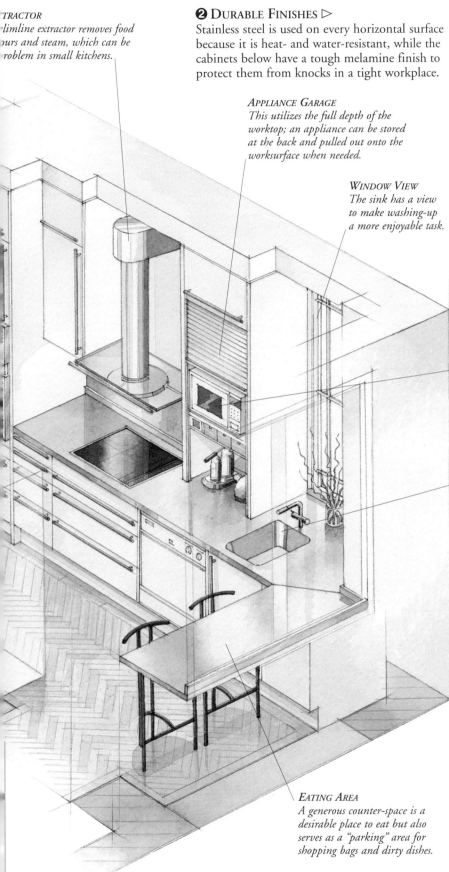

FOR MORE DETAILS...

Appliance garage SEE P. 24

Halogen hob SEE P. 28

Eye-level double oven SEE P. 31

Bar eating SEE P. 32

Stainless steel worktops SEE P. 38

SINGLE SINK
A small sink saves on precious worktop space. Use it for washing food, and rinsing dishes before placing them in the dishwasher below.

EATING AREA
A generous counter-space is a desirable place to eat but also serves as a "parking" area for shopping bags and dirty dishes.

WOOD FLOORING
A natural beech floor adds warmth and offsets the hard, industrial finishes used elsewhere.

❸ NATURAL LIGHT ▷

The light-reflective qualities of stainless steel, together with an open undercounter space and tall windows, make this end of the kitchen feel both light and airy.

SMALL KITCHEN CHOICE

△ MAXIMIZING FLOOR SPACE

A handmade kitchen can be an efficient choice, as furniture can be tailor-made to fit the space. Here, the major appliances sit in a tall stack, while the area beneath the hob is kept free to make the kitchen feel spacious.

FORM FOLLOWS FUNCTION ▷

A straight run of units is arranged in a clear, logical sequence, with the sink between the hob and food preparation area. Above and below counter level, well-designed cupboards offer distinct open and closed storage areas.

◁ KITCHENS WITHOUT WINDOWS

Every available space from floor to ceiling has been filled in this tiny kitchen without windows. Strong task lighting, a simple palette of materials, cool colours, and open shelving produce a calm, well-ordered result.

MOVING IN CIRCLES ▷

A circular kitchen fits comfortably into a room 2.9m (9ft 6in) wide. The centralized arrangement of activities, with the cook in the middle, makes movement between different work stations highly efficient.

UNFITTED KITCHEN PLAN

UNLIKE FITTED KITCHENS in which standard units run from wall to wall, the unfitted kitchen takes a less formal approach. It is home to a collection of hand-crafted pieces that stand alone, and although the sink cabinet is still "technically" fitted, the overall effect is of individual elements with separate tasks, working together to create a smooth-running whole.

△ ❶ CLOSE PROXIMITY
The cooking and preparation zones occupy their own distinct areas within the kitchen but sit only two steps away from one another, for maximum efficiency.

DESIGN POINTS

■ Imagine activity and storage areas as separate pieces of free-standing furniture. Buy items from a variety of sources and enjoy the differences of shape, height, colour, and finish that each item has to offer.

■ Retain or uncover existing architectural features, such as fireplaces and alcoves, to add character to the room.

■ Where possible, allow space around each piece of furniture, but make sure all the essential facilities are conveniently close to one another. Try to keep the cooking and food preparation areas as the focus of the room.

COURT CUPBOARD
Decorative cabinetry, mounted on a platform, conceals a raised-height fridge-freezer.

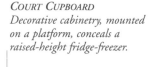

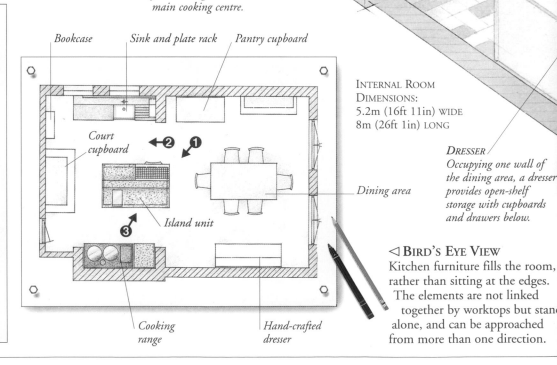

AGA
Self-contained in its own tiled alcove, this five-door Aga is the main cooking centre.

Bookcase   Sink and plate rack   Pantry cupboard

Court cupboard

←❷ ❶↘

❸↗

Island unit

Cooking range

Hand-crafted dresser

INTERNAL ROOM DIMENSIONS:
5.2m (16ft 11in) WIDE
8m (26ft 1in) LONG

DRESSER
Occupying one wall of the dining area, a dresser provides open-shelf storage with cupboards and drawers below.

Dining area

◁ BIRD'S EYE VIEW
Kitchen furniture fills the room, rather than sitting at the edges. The elements are not linked together by worktops but stand alone, and can be approached from more than one direction.

BOOKSHELVES
A wall-mounted bookcase, with a wine rack below utilizes the corner space without making the room feel overcrowded.

❷ CONTRASTING ELEMENTS ▷
Standing side by side, the difference in height, style, and finish between the court cupboard and the bookshelf emphasizes the separate functions of these pieces of furniture, while enhancing the furnished, living-room feel of the room.

CENTRAL ISLAND
The chopping and food preparation area is divided up into granite and end-grain wood surfaces at different heights.

PANTRY CUPBOARD
Space in front of the unit ensures that the wide doors can be left open when re-stocking.

FOR MORE DETAILS...

Pantry cupboard SEE PP. 18–19

Fridge-freezer SEE PP. 20–21

Aga SEE P. 30

Rectangular table SEE P. 33

Tiles SEE PP. 42–43

PARLOUR CUPBOARD
Wall-mounted to free the floor space around the eating area, this custom-made unit stores china, table linen, and breakfast cereals.

FRENCH WINDOWS
Next to the eating area, large windows provide natural light and a view of the garden.

REFECTORY TABLE
Generous space around the table allows up to ten people to enjoy a meal in comfort.

TERRACOTTA TILES
Large, reclaimed terracotta tiles provide atmosphere and durability.

❸ STORAGE FACILITIES ▷
A tall pantry cupboard rather than a row of base and wall units is an efficient use of space. Everyday crockery sits on a wall-mounted plate rack, and baskets hang on hooks from a gantry.

UNFITTED KITCHEN CHOICE

△ SIMPLE STAND-ALONE FURNITURE
The simplicity of freestanding kitchen furniture is very appealing, and here the combination of painted wood and white walls adds to the effect. The space around each item is important, so avoid continuous runs of units, to prevent cluttering up every wall and corner.

△ ROOM DIVIDERS
In an unfitted kitchen, there is more scope to use old pieces of furniture. The antique pine dresser in the foreground acts as a room divider, separating off the cooking and eating areas. New cabinets provide worktops and storage facilities close to the Aga cooker.

RETAINING ORIGINAL FEATURES ▷
A well-furnished kitchen can combine both freestanding and built-in items successfully. Here, a sitting room was converted to make a large kitchen. Some features were kept intact, such as the ceiling mouldings and the chimney breast; the hob and oven sit in this alcove and use the flue for ventilation.

△ APPLIANCES BEHIND DOORS
A well-proportioned court cupboard can be an attractive and convenient home for large appliances. In this kitchen, a fridge and microwave are built into the cupboard but it could just as easily contain an eye-level oven and a larder for fresh and non-perishable foods.

△ ACCESSIBLE STORAGE
The most useful storage space sits between knee height and eye level; in one large cupboard the space offered at this level is greater than in a series of units above and below worktops. Above all, a tall cupboard is a feature and a relief from the uniformity of similar-height cabinets.

FITTED KITCHEN PLAN

IMAGINATION AND resourcefulness are needed to design a kitchen using standard fitted units. The secret is to be selective, so that your kitchen is not overwhelmed by repetitive cabinetry. Pick doors, drawers, and glass-fronted units from a standard range, and then shop around for worktops, flooring, and lighting to reflect personal taste.

BLACKBOARD
A leftover cabinet door has been coated in blackboard paint to create a message board.

WALLCOVERING
A cream, oil-based paint lightens the room and is easy to wipe clean.

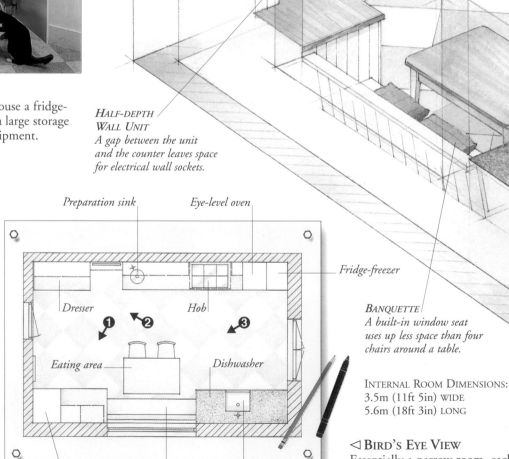

△ ❶ UTILITY CUPBOARD
A tall two-door unit, designed to house a fridge-freezer, has been adapted to create a large storage cupboard for essential cleaning equipment.

HALF-DEPTH WALL UNIT
A gap between the unit and the counter leaves space for electrical wall sockets.

DESIGN POINTS

■ Try to create visual interest by avoiding very long runs of similar cabinets with the same door fronts. Break up the monotony by leaving wall space for shelves and pictures.

■ Consider how to balance the horizontal and vertical lines in a unit kitchen. Blocks of tall cabinets, adjacent to the wall, can remove the tyranny of long counters and wall units.

■ To make a fitted kitchen less clinical, try customizing units. Employ a carpenter to build a dresser above base units or, as a cheaper alternative, adapt existing carcasses and paint the insides in bright colours.

Preparation sink   Eye-level oven

Dresser   *Hob*

❶ ❷ ❸

Eating area

Utility cupboard   *Bench seat*   *Porcelain sink*

Fridge-freezer

BANQUETTE
A built-in window seat uses up less space than four chairs around a table.

Dishwasher

INTERNAL ROOM DIMENSIONS:
3.5m (11ft 5in) WIDE
5.6m (18ft 3in) LONG

◁ BIRD'S EYE VIEW
Essentially a narrow room, each long wall is intensively used, but clever elevations underlie what in the plan looks like a plain row of units.

CUSTOM-MADE DRESSER
The top of the dresser is edged with leftover wood moulding, for decoration.

TEA-TOWEL RACK
A hanging rack is a useful device to fill a wall left intentionally free of units.

VEGETABLE SINK
Fresh ingredients can be rinsed at the preparation site, preventing a journey across the kitchen.

FOR MORE DETAILS...

Vegetable sink SEE P. 26

Lacquered wood worktops SEE P. 39

Linoleum floor SEE P. 45

Ceiling downlights SEE P. 46

EXTRACTOR AND HOB
The choice of a stylish aluminium extractor hood and five- rather than four-ring hob helps personalize this fitted kitchen range.

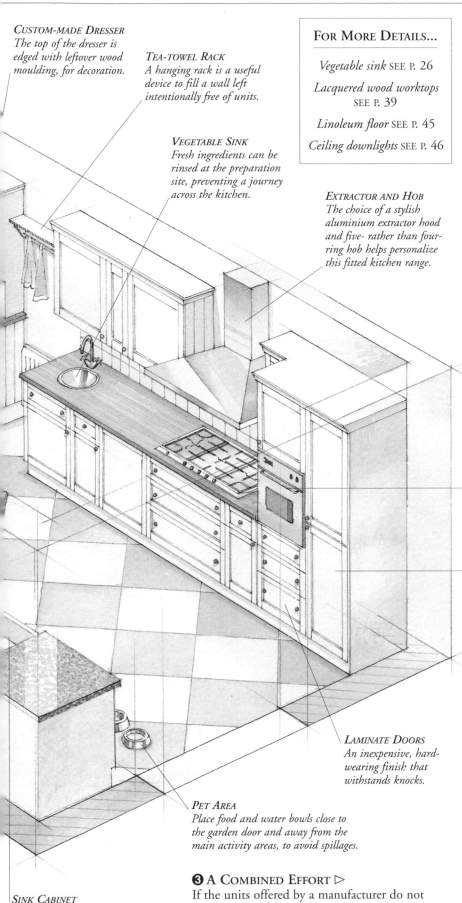

△ ❷ **ATTENTION TO DETAIL**
Simple additions can make all the difference. Here, a dresser has been built on top of a standard unit, and thin beech worktops are edged with 40mm (1½in) strips to make them look more solid.

EYE-LEVEL OVEN
Place a storage cupboard above and drawers below to vary the appearance of the cabinets.

REFRIGERATOR HOUSING
The oven and fridge sit next to one another and must be well insulated to save energy.

LAMINATE DOORS
An inexpensive, hard-wearing finish that withstands knocks.

PET AREA
Place food and water bowls close to the garden door and away from the main activity areas, to avoid spillages.

❸ **A COMBINED EFFORT** ▷
If the units offered by a manufacturer do not match your needs, commission a handmade piece of kitchen furniture to your specification, as in the case of this space-saving window seat.

SINK CABINET
The sink is fitted into a standard carcass, but durable granite worktops add individuality.

FITTED KITCHEN CHOICE

△ BOLD PLANNING

The design of this kitchen brings the fitted units into the centre of the room rather than placing them around the walls. The hob and sink face one another so that the cook can enjoy two different views when working. Painted plaster walls offset cool stainless steel.

△ STANDARD FITTED UNITS

A low-budget kitchen uses a standard row of base units to create maximum worktop and storage space. The large preparation area has been adapted to suit the cook's needs by adding a small sink for rinsing fresh foods.

QUALITY AND COMFORT ▷

Manufactured to a high specification, using durable, hygienic materials such as ceramic floor tiles, granite and stainless steel, this fitted kitchen is built to last. It combines high-tech materials with wood, to add the comfort associated with country kitchens.

△ BEHIND CLOSED DOORS

The choice of all-white matching finishes on the fitted cabinetry and walls helps to brighten up this narrow kitchen, which is annexed off a larger room. Eye level, wall-mounted cabinets have been abandoned in favour of floor-to-ceiling cupboards along the entrance corridor.

△ COLOUR VARIATION

The units have been carefully chosen from a standard range so that they fit imaginatively into the room plan. A run of base cabinets surrounds the eating area and doubles up as a serving counter. Their bright painted blue finish adds character to the room, which can be difficult to achieve in fitted kitchens.

ISLAND KITCHEN PLAN

A CENTRAL ISLAND is the key to a large, sociable kitchen because the cook is able to look into the room rather than at a blank wall. In spatial terms, an island arrangement helps to concentrate cooking activities into a small zone so that the cook does not have to waste time travelling backwards and forwards across the entire room.

Cupboard   *Sink*   *Dishwasher and back-up oven*

INTERNAL ROOM DIMENSIONS:
4.7m (15ft 4in) WIDE
6.4m (20ft 10in) LONG

③

①

Fridge

Dresser

Island unit

Sofa

②

Eating area

△ BIRD'S EYE VIEW

For an island to be successful, it needs space around it. Allow 1.2m (3ft 10in) between the island and the wall cabinets. If a sink is directly behind the work area, ensure there is at least 1m (3ft 3in) so that two people can work back to back.

DESIGN POINTS

■ Allow space between key activities on the island – the wooden chopping block and gas hob should be 45cm (18in) apart to prevent heat damage and fire risk.

■ Plan a low-level worktop for operating electrical appliances on the island. If finished in cold marble or granite, it can double up as a pastry area.

■ Lighting is important in a kitchen used for both cooking and entertaining. Ensure that the island is well lit from above so that you are not working in shadow, and install lights on dimmer switches to create a soft, ambient light in eating and relaxation areas.

PLATE RACK
A wall-mounted rack drip-dries and stores wet plates direct from the dishwasher or adjacent sink.

LARGE SINK
A deep sink is suitable for soaking oven pans, while heavy pots need only be carried a short distance from the hob for draining.

CHOPPING BLOCK
Positioned with a view of the table and garden beyond, the chopping block is within reach of the sink, hob, and fridge.

STORAGE CUPBOARD
Bulky hardware is stored just behind the island.

LOW-LEVEL COUNTER
Built-in electrical sockets make it possible to use food processors and other electrical appliances on the island.

◁ ❶ SOCIABLE COOKING

The gas hob and below-deck oven are orientated towards the blue sofa so that the cook can talk to guests. A stainless steel upturn at the back protects the lacquered serving counter from oil and sauces.

DISHWASHER STACK
An eye-level oven sits on top of a raised dishwasher to reduce the need to bend.

➋ EYE-CATCHING CABINETRY ▷
The serving counter cabinet is the most decorative of the four island zones, as it is seen from the table. It hides the hob, making it easier to cook in front of an audience without inhibition.

FULL-HEIGHT FRIDGE
The island plan frees up space around the walls for a large fridge a short distance from the preparation area.

STAINLESS STEEL HOB
The worktops that flank the hob are heatproof. Allow at least 30cm (12in) on either side.

FOR MORE DETAILS...

Centre island unit
SEE PP. 24–25

Hobs and extractors
SEE PP. 28–29

Storage cupboard SEE P. 36

Lighting SEE PP. 46–47

WINDOWS
A wall of windows, plus glass doors leading to the garden, fill the room with light.

KITCHEN TABLE
Planned in the brightest corner of the kitchen, the family table has an oiled wood surface to make it hardwearing.

SERVING AREA
A free counter for serving food, between the cooking zone and the table, makes entertaining easy.

RELAXATION AREA
Space for a sitting area is made possible by focusing appliances and worktops in the centre of the kitchen.

➌ FULL PARTICIPATION ▷
Trips back to the hob mid-meal to perform the finishing touches to a dish are no longer a chore as the cook is not excluded from round-table talks.

ISLAND KITCHEN CHOICE

△ MINIMALIST ISLAND FITTING
A brushed stainless steel island unit with a small, moulded sink, gives the extrovert cook the necessary facilities to wash and prepare fresh ingredients while entertaining guests, who can perch on stools at the other side.

VARIABLE-HEIGHT ISLAND ▷
A central island works best if it has been divided into four key activity zones, each arranged at the most efficient height to perform the required tasks. Unlike most fitted kitchens, where long runs of worktops are arranged around the kitchen walls, the island enables you to occupy centre stage.

△ MULTI-FUNCTIONAL PENINSULAR UNIT
In a small kitchen, where worktop space is limited and there is no room for a table, consider a circular half end-grain wood and half granite peninsular unit. The purpose-built fitting doubles up as a food preparation and eating area without taking up valuable floor space.

△ CENTRAL WASHING-UP AREA
If your kitchen has no spectacular window view, build the sink into an island unit so that you can face the room rather than a blank wall when performing this mundane task. Here, the sink is thoughtfully placed so that you simply turn around to use the hob.

△ SLENDER ISLAND WORKING TABLE WITH RAISED-HEIGHT PLATFORM
A narrow kitchen can accommodate a long modern or traditional working table that acts as a central workspace for several people at once. A removable preparation platform at one end of the table allows you to stand and prepare meals while supervising children's activities.

IMPROVISED KITCHEN PLAN

ONCE YOU UNDERSTAND the principles of ergonomic kitchen design, it is possible to assemble a comfortable and easy-to-use kitchen on a tight budget. The secret is to improvise, so rather than just settling for low-cost units, scour junk shops and auctions for furniture that can be adapted for kitchen use, and bring inherited items, which you may have placed elsewhere in your home, into the kitchen.

APOTHECARY DRAWERS
Drawers picked up at auction store spices, candles, and other household items.

PORCELAIN SINK
Inherited intact, this porcelain sink with drainer attached is built into a homemade kitchen cabinet.

△ ❶ CONTAINED SPACE
As space is limited, the sink, cooker, and preparation area butt up against one another, but this compact arrangement works well.

HARDWARE STORAGE
A china cupboard and cutlery drawer below the sink allow items to be put away as soon as they have been washed up.

WOODEN BENCH
With no room for a table, a bench provides a place for guests to sit.

DESIGN POINTS

■ Thoughtful selection of items is necessary; ensure that they are functional and measure each piece of furniture to check that there is room for them.

■ The most problematic area is around the sink. Think about the amount of draining board space – allow 60cm (24in) on either side. Consider how the worktop joins up to the basin – it needs a high-performance seal. Also, the area behind the sink needs protecting from watersplashes (*see pp.42–43*).

■ Finding furniture with hardwearing worktops may be difficult. Assess your priorities to see whether you can install new worktops (*see pp.38–39*).

INTERNAL ROOM DIMENSIONS:
1.9m (6ft 2in) WIDE
4.7m (15ft 4in) LONG

Spice drawers

Cooker unit   *Food preparation area*

❸ ❷   ←❶

Sink cabinet   *Bench*

Small cupboard

Waist-height storage cupboard

Wood-burning stove

◁ BIRD'S EYE VIEW
The sink, cooker, and a long food preparation counter form an L-shape of fitted cabinetry, while unfitted cupboards and a bench sit up close, leaving space for the sink cabinet doors to open.

FREESTANDING GAS COOKER
This upright gas appliance has
a fold-away grill at eye level.
Easy-to-watch, eye-level grills
are only found on old cookers.

UNDERCOUNTER FRIDGE
Fitted below the preparation
area, a small fridge squeezes
into a narrow space, and is
cheap to buy secondhand.

FOR MORE DETAILS...

Undercounter fridge
SEE P. 20

Oven cooking SEE P. 30

Sink cabinet SEE P. 34

Wallcoverings
SEE PP. 42–43

STORAGE SHELF
An old pine shelf provides open
storage above the counter for
utensils and equipment, and
keeps the worktop space free.

△ ❷ PROTECTIVE MEASURES
In this narrow kitchen, the wood counter butts up
against the cooker. To keep the wood surface intact,
hot pans are always put down on heatproof mats.

ASPECT
Clever planning means that the
worktop sits between two windows
and is flooded with natural light.

WOOD-BURNING STOVE
A cast-iron stove provides extra
"parking" space for items close
to the food preparation counter.

TERRACOTTA TILES
Tiles, bought from an old
farmhouse and cleaned,
make a durable flooring.

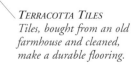

❸ LOW-COST MATERIALS ▷
Painted wood boarding is employed to great
effect to cover up an uneven ceiling. It is also
used to build low-cost fitted cabinetry below
the sink unit and the wood worktops.

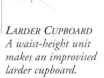

LARDER CUPBOARD
A waist-height unit
makes an improvised
larder cupboard.

IMPROVISED KITCHEN CHOICE

△ AFFORDABLE STAINLESS STEEL
If you like the qualities of stainless steel but cannot afford new units, try a catering auction where secondhand professional kitchen fittings are sold. Try to purchase a stainless steel workbench and a sink to provide a basic washing-up, food preparation, and bar eating area.

△ EQUIPMENT RACKS
Utensils hanging on the wall not only look attractive but are stored within easy reach of the counter. Here, three stainless steel towel rails have been installed to make a hanging device. For a longer worktop, try using a coat rail taken from an old wardrobe.

WALL DISPLAY ▷
In small, narrow kitchens, there is often not the room for a desk in which to store meal plans or lists of household tasks. Instead, put up a noticeboard and attach favourite recipes, food lists, and bills for safe keeping.

△ INEXPENSIVE FACELIFT
If it is not within your budget to alter the plan of your kitchen to suit your specific needs, transform its appearance by painting the cabinets in a strong colour and changing the door handles. On a bigger budget, new worktops and lighting make a huge difference.

△ DO-IT-YOURSELF SHELVING
Open shelves fitted with hooks are relatively easy to construct and have the capacity to store a variety of kitchen equipment above counter level. Although a less expensive alternative to purpose-built cabinets, items stored in this way will gather dust and need to be brought down regularly for cleaning.

FAMILY KITCHEN PLAN

A FAMILY KITCHEN is more than just a place for cooking food, and here lies the challenge. It is the centre of family life and should be arranged accordingly. Divide the room into distinct zones: an island cooking area, where the cook faces into the room as he or she works; an informal eating area; and a play and relaxation area with a large sofa.

DESIGN POINTS

■ Make sure that you are happy cooking in front of an audience before you opt for an open-plan family kitchen.

■ Use soft furnishings, such as sofas and rugs, to absorb sound and so help to reduce noise levels in a large family kitchen.

■ A long island works best if you plan two circular food preparation areas at either end.

■ Position the sink and hob opposite one another, to minimize walking distances.

■ Allow room for plenty of storage space and ensure that it is in easy reach of activity areas.

PANTRY CUPBOARD
A full-height food storage cupboard – rather than storage above and below the counter – caters for family needs.

FIREPLACE
As units and appliances are not spread around the whole room, a fireplace can be integrated into the plan.

CEILING LIGHTS
Disc lights hang down on stems from the ceiling, helping to lower the ceiling height and so create a more intimate atmosphere at night.

SITTING AREA
Sofa and chair are grouped around the fireplace to create a "soft" area for relaxing and playing.

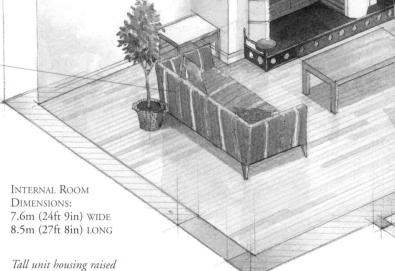

INTERNAL ROOM
DIMENSIONS:
7.6m (24ft 9in) WIDE
8.5m (27ft 8in) LONG

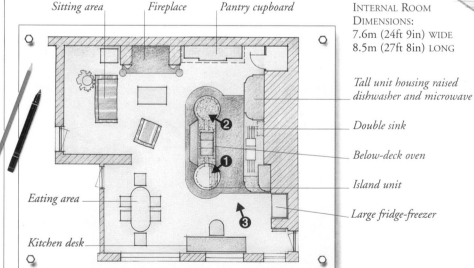

Sitting area   Fireplace   Pantry cupboard

Eating area

Kitchen desk

Tall unit housing raised dishwasher and microwave

Double sink

Below-deck oven

Island unit

Large fridge-freezer

△ **BIRD'S EYE VIEW**
Appliances are confined to the island and sink cabinet to keep cooking activities close together, while freeing up space elsewhere for an eating and sitting area.

❶ **SUPERVISED ACTIVITIES** ▷
An unobstructed view from the island to the oval table means that homework, drawing, and other table-top activities can be supervised while food is prepared.

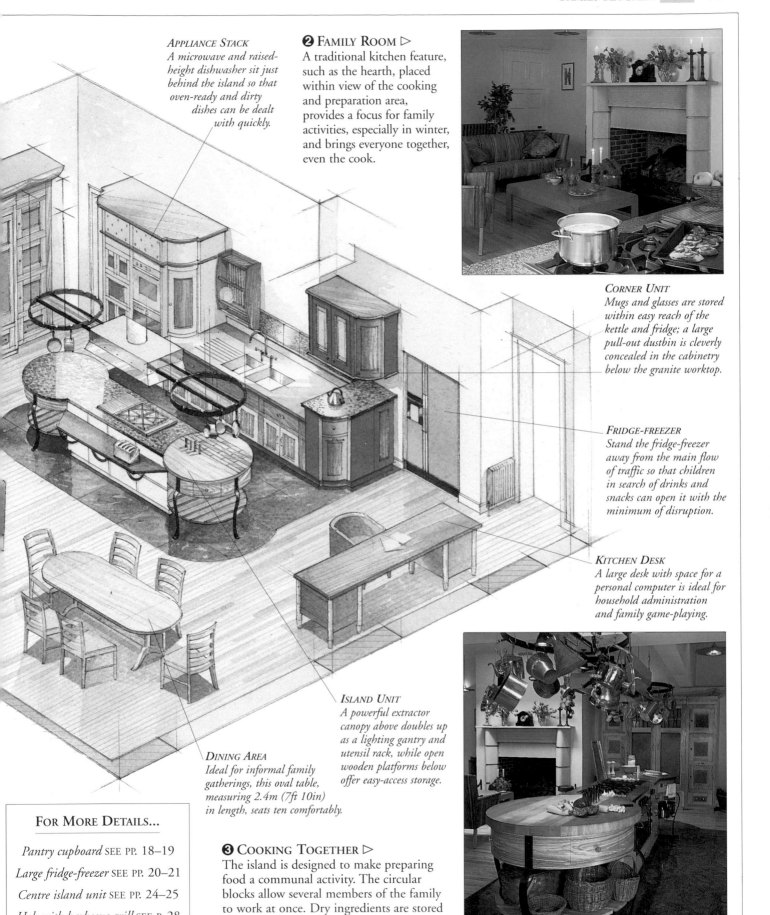

APPLIANCE STACK
A microwave and raised-height dishwasher sit just behind the island so that oven-ready and dirty dishes can be dealt with quickly.

❷ FAMILY ROOM ▷
A traditional kitchen feature, such as the hearth, placed within view of the cooking and preparation area, provides a focus for family activities, especially in winter, and brings everyone together, even the cook.

CORNER UNIT
Mugs and glasses are stored within easy reach of the kettle and fridge; a large pull-out dustbin is cleverly concealed in the cabinetry below the granite worktop.

FRIDGE-FREEZER
Stand the fridge-freezer away from the main flow of traffic so that children in search of drinks and snacks can open it with the minimum of disruption.

KITCHEN DESK
A large desk with space for a personal computer is ideal for household administration and family game-playing.

ISLAND UNIT
A powerful extractor canopy above doubles up as a lighting gantry and utensil rack, while open wooden platforms below offer easy-access storage.

DINING AREA
Ideal for informal family gatherings, this oval table, measuring 2.4m (7ft 10in) in length, seats ten comfortably.

FOR MORE DETAILS...

Pantry cupboard SEE PP. 18–19

Large fridge-freezer SEE PP. 20–21

Centre island unit SEE PP. 24–25

Hob with barbecue grill SEE P. 28

Oval table SEE P. 33

❸ COOKING TOGETHER ▷
The island is designed to make preparing food a communal activity. The circular blocks allow several members of the family to work at once. Dry ingredients are stored in the pantry, close to the granite pastry-making block. Fresh food is kept in the fridge, a few paces from the end-grain block.

FAMILY KITCHEN CHOICE

△ EATING TOGETHER

The kitchen table is the focal point of family life, so even when space is limited, try to include a table in your plan. A small, round table, 1.2m (3ft 10in) in diameter seats four. When not in use, the chairs can be tucked in closer to the table.

CREATIVE ACTIVITIES ▷

A family kitchen table is not only used at mealtimes but for a variety of activities, such as painting, drawing, and model-making. Choose an old pine table where blemishes will not be too obvious, or cover the table with a waterproof tablecloth for protection.

△ CHILDREN'S COOKING SHELF

The low slate shelf that runs along the front edge of the island provides an indestructible child-height counter for younger members of the family who enjoy cooking. At other times, it functions as a preparation centre for operating electrical appliances, and a breakfast bar.

△ TOY DRAWER

Toys scattered all over the floor are likely to cause accidents, so plan a pull-out drawer where toys can be quickly stowed away as mealtime approaches. A hygienic floor covering, such as linoleum, is also advisable.

△ KITCHEN OFFICE

A desk area in the kitchen can be useful for organizing both household administration and helping children with their homework while you are involved in kitchen tasks. A pinboard and blackboard for notes and shopping lists also help your household to run smoothly.

MADE IN ENGLAND
unique 24108

PLOT YOUR ROOM

THE FLOOR PLAN and elevations are the starting point for any new kitchen design. Use the following simple step-by-step guide to help you map out a survey of the room, and then to transfer your measurements onto graph paper to create accurate scale drawings.

COLOURED PENCILS

RUBBER

NOTEPAD

CAMERA

STEP LADDER

TAPE MEASURE

EQUIPMENT
To help you create an accurate visual record of the room's dimensions, fixed service points, and awkward architectural features, you will need this basic equipment.

FLOOR DIMENSIONS

Before you begin work on a new kitchen design, you must familiarize yourself with the features of the room that you have chosen as your kitchen. Accurate measurements of the floor area will help you work out whether an appliance or item of furniture will fit comfortably into the available space, while a survey of service points, natural light sources, outside walls, and kitchen access will help you to plan the best location for food preparation, cooking, eating, and washing-up areas in your new kitchen.

❶ SKETCH THE ROOM
Stand in the middle of the room and look down at the floor. Hand-draw a rough sketch of the floor area in a notepad with a soft pencil. Draw in the shapes of fixed furniture or architectural features to be incorporated into your new design.

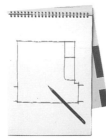

❷ PLOT THE DIMENSIONS
Next, measure the total floor area. Place the tape measure across the room, and note down the length on your sketch in coloured pencil or pen. At this stage, it is simpler to ignore surface details, such as skirting boards, in your calculations.

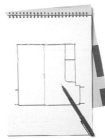

❸ PLOT THE WALLS
Following the room round in a clockwise direction, so as not to confuse yourself, measure each wall length in turn. Do not assume that the walls are symmetrical, and carefully mark down the measurements on your sketch for future reference.

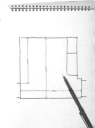

❹ PLOT SERVICE POINTS
Survey the room for service points, such as gas and water supply, and electrical sockets. If present, plot their position on your survey. Indicate structural features to be incorporated into the design – chimney flues, outside walls, and room orientation.

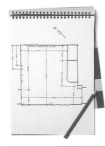

❺ PLOT FIXED FEATURES
Measure the dimensions and position in the room of any appliances or cabinetry you do not wish to move, such as an Aga or store cupboard, and then draw them onto your sketch. Remember though, most items are fairly inexpensive to relocate.

❻ PHOTOGRAPH ODD CORNERS
Take photographs to help you record areas where it is hard to measure the dimensions, perhaps in awkward corners or on sloping walls. Photographs of features in the room, such as fireplaces, will also help you to recall style details when designing a new kitchen.

WALL ELEVATIONS

Although you do not need very detailed elevations to design your new kitchen, it is useful to have a sketch survey of each of the four walls. These sketches help to establish whether there is enough wall space for freestanding furniture without blocking windows, radiators, or other fixed features. With elevations, you can also envisage what size of furniture would best suit the proportions of the room.

❶ MEASURE THE HEIGHT
Stand facing one wall and draw a rough sketch of it. Draw in doors, windows, or alcoves. Architectural details, such as mouldings, are not yet important. Stand on a step ladder and measure the wall height from floor to ceiling. Note it on the sketch.

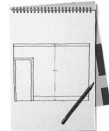

❷ MEASURE THE DOORS
Record the height and width of any doors, skirting boards, and cornices, plus the details of any surrounding frames or decorative mouldings. Note the dimensions of the service points that you may not wish to obstruct. Draw an elevation sketch for each wall.

DRAWING UP SCALE PLANS

The rough sketch survey of the existing room plan (see p.76) contains all the information you need to work out where appliances and furniture can be placed within your new kitchen. However, if you wish to take the design further, you may want to draw up the plan and elevations to scale. Follow the instructions below.

GRAPH PAPER

SET SQUARE

INK PEN

50CM RULER

OUTSIDE WALLS
A thick border of cross-hatching indicates outside walls.

YOU WILL NEED
Metric and imperial graph paper is supplied with this book but you will also need the equipment shown above.

◁ **❶ TRANSFER THE FLOOR PLAN**
Refer to your rough plan for precise measurements, and then accurately plot the four perimeter walls to scale on graph paper. Join up straight lines with a set square. Next, plot key features such as outside walls, doors, and windows that are important for planning your new kitchen.

DOOR HINGING
A dotted line indicates the direction in which the door swings open.

LIGHT
Parallel lines show a window as a light source.

CORNICE HEIGHT
The width of the cornice will limit the height of tall cabinetry.

❷ DRAW UP AN ELEVATION ▷
Referring to the measurements on your sketch elevations, draw up each wall to scale. Work from the floor upwards, marking on details and services last.

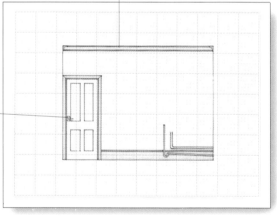

DOOR KNOB
Indicate the way the door opens by drawing on the door handle.

❸ OTHER ELEVATIONS ▽
Draw each of the remaining elevations to scale, marking on relevant details to give you a complete picture of the room before you begin the design.

WINDOWS
Include details such as moulding and windowsill measurements.

SKIRTING BOARD
A thicker line distinguishes the skirting board from the floor line.

THE WHOLE PICTURE
For accuracy, draw in the radiator, skirting board, and the side of a cupboard seen from this viewpoint.

PLACE THE FEATURES

REFER TO THE LIST you have compiled of your chosen kitchen appliances, furniture, and materials, and you should have all the information you require to plan a kitchen that suits your personality and needs. The next step is to find a successful way of arranging the features in your designated space. Try out several different arrangements by placing a piece of tracing paper over the scaled-up room plan (*see pp.76–77*), and drawing on the elements, following the order of design (*see right*). You may draw several versions before reaching the best solution.

TRACING PAPER

MASKING TAPE

SET SQUARE

YOU WILL NEED ▷
Take the room plan that you have drawn to scale, and stick a sheet of tracing paper over the top with masking tape. Place the features using a soft pencil, ruler, and set square. When you want to explore a new design, start afresh on a clean sheet of tracing paper.

PEN
PENCIL
RUBBER

RULER

ORDER OF DESIGN

When designing your new kitchen layout, place your chosen elements on the room plan in the following order, to avoid confusion.

❶ **PLACE THE SINK CABINET** first on your plan because, including draining boards, it is the longest unit. Arrange the cooking area, preparation area, and dishwasher close by.

❷ **POSITION THE HOB** a few steps from the sink so that you can deal with pans without having to walk across the kitchen. Consider where to place a high- or low-level oven.

❸ **PLAN THE PREPARATION AREA** within reach of the hob but also a short distance from the sink for rinsing fresh ingredients.

❹ **PLACE THE FRIDGE** away from the main area of traffic around the sink, but close to the preparation zone and kitchen table.

❺ **POSITION THE TABLE** near a natural light source and away from activity areas. Plan wall-mounted and below-counter storage facilities within reach of activity centres.

REJECTED PLANS

Arriving at a well-planned, ergonomic design takes time, especially if the room contains fixed features that have to be incorporated into the design. Let your kitchen plan evolve, and learn from the designs that you reject in the process.

REDUCED STORAGE ▽
The worktop space is increased by a peninsular unit, but the fridge is now across the room. The table sits under the window but the large cupboard has been halved in size to make space.

SINK AREA
The corner space is crowded but food preparation area is greater.

RESTRICTED ACCESS ▽
A double sink and dining area are planned but both are crowded. The sink faces the wall and is overhung by wall units, while the fridge door and table restrict access to the room.

WALL UNITS
Eye-level units over the sink make this corner feel cramped.

EATING AREA
The table only seats three and projects into the room, blocking the entrance.

CHOPPING BLOCK
There is only room for a small food preparation area between hob and fridge.

FULL-HEIGHT FRIDGE
This tall unit obstructs your eyeline on entering the kitchen.

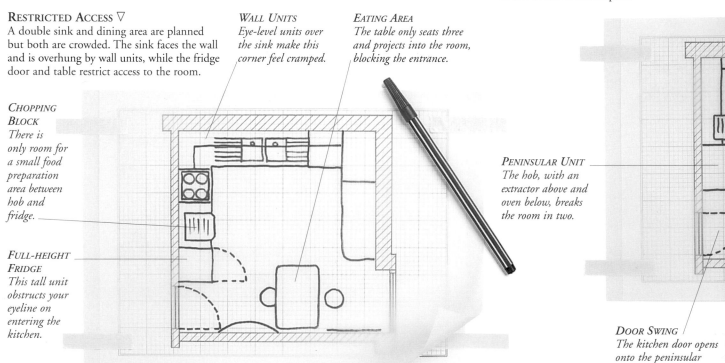

PENINSULAR UNIT
The hob, with an extractor above and oven below, breaks the room in two.

DOOR SWING
The kitchen door opens onto the peninsular unit, crowding entry.

SUCCESSFUL PLAN

Having resolved how best to arrange the appliances within the space, and if satisfied that you have found an ergonomic solution, plot your final design onto graph paper in ink pen.

NEW WINDOW
This is installed in an outside wall to create access to natural light for the double sink.

RAISED-HEIGHT DISHWASHER
Placed between the sink and a built-in cupboard, dishes are rinsed before washing and then put away afterwards.

BOILER CUPBOARD
The boiler cannot be moved and so this corner unit has to be fitted into the design.

HOB AND BELOW-COUNTER OVEN
These appliances are surrounded by a heat-resistant granite worktop and are within reach of the sink.

BUILT-IN CUPBOARD
An original cupboard is left intact, and is adapted to house both a full-height fridge and china storage.

PREPARATION AREA
A circular half end-grain and granite block provides a generous worktop close to the hob without breaking up the room space.

TELEPHONE SHELF
A narrow ledge fixed onto the cupboard is a useful space for a telephone, within reach of the table.

DOOR OPENING
Rehung so that it opens against the right-hand wall, it allows an open view of the kitchen. Also, more than one person can prepare food at the circle without having to close the door first.

WINDOW
The original window lights this end of the room.

WALL SHELVES
A narrow set of curved shelves fit on the wall between the door and table without taking up valuable floor space.

SMALL TABLE
Pushed against the wall close to the window to save space, it can be pulled out to seat four.

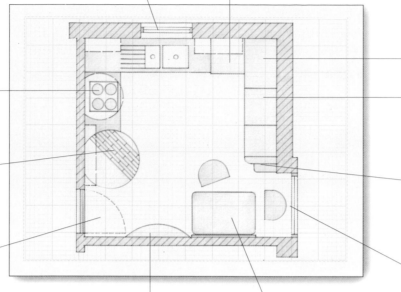

LIMITED WORKTOPS ▽
The sink cabinet fits next to the window but journeys from the sink to the hob are interrupted by people entering and leaving the room. Floor-to-ceiling storage units take priority over worktops, which comprise only a small area by the hob.

EATING AREA
Poorly placed at the dark end of the room, the table is surrounded by tall cabinets.

CENTRAL SPACE
There is too much unused space in the centre, due to poor planning.

STORAGE
A cupboard above the dishwasher, a plate rack, and shelves, provide minimum storage.

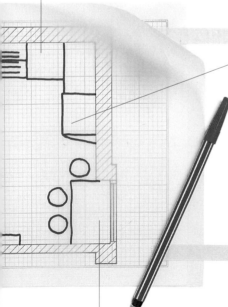

FULL-HEIGHT FRIDGE
This is housed in the remaining half of the built-in cupboard.

WORKTOP
There is only space for a small worktop next to the hob for food preparation.

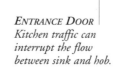

TABLE IN WINDOW
A fixed table is inflexible and part of the built-in cupboard has been removed to make room for seats.

ENTRANCE DOOR
Kitchen traffic can interrupt the flow between sink and hob.

APPLIANCE STACK
An oven and dishwasher stack near the door crowds the entrance.

PLANNING DETAIL

WHEN YOU HAVE arrived at a satisfactory floor plan, you can start to consider the finer details. Choose cabinet finishes, wallcoverings, flooring, and lighting that match your kitchen needs, but bear in mind your budget, and the amount of time you have allowed for the work.

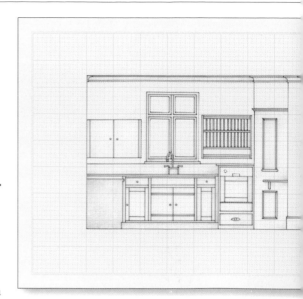

◁ **COLLECT PHOTOGRAPHS**
You may already have chosen specific appliances and cabinets to fit limited floor space but if not, pictures from magazines and catalogues will help you clarify the style you favour, whether traditional, modern, or high-tech.

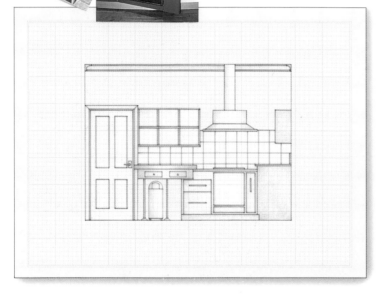

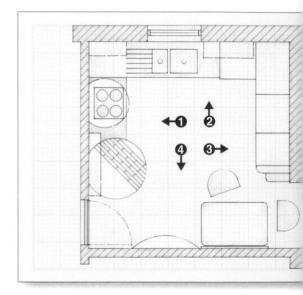

△ ❶ **COOKING AND PREPARATION ZONE**
Draw in outline wall-mounted and below-counter units to see in detail how they fit into the existing space. Here, two shallow drawers in the preparation table hold utensils, while a rubbish bin sits between its legs. Deep pan drawers and a tall, single drawer for cooking oils flank the oven.

❹ **BOOKSHELF AND TABLE** ▷
The door opens onto the right-hand wall so this area is kept simple to avoid obstructing the entrance. Select a sturdy, wall-mounted bookshelf, noticeboard, kitchen table, and wall-covering, on the basis that this area of the room may be susceptible to knocks.

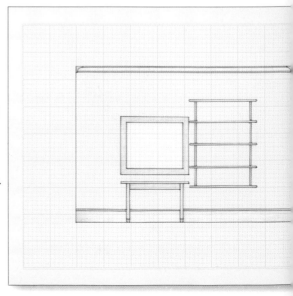

◁ **STORE SAMPLES**
Collect paint colour, tile, and worktop samples from DIY and interior design shops to help you build up a picture of your finished kitchen.

REFER TO CATALOGUES ▷
Keep the catalogues that feature your chosen appliances and materials to hand, to help you cost the project and as a source of local stockists and suppliers for placing your orders.

◁ ❷ SINK ELEVATION
Focus on the sink cabinet and pay attention to detail, such as the choice of materials for the sink basin, cabinet doors, taps, draining boards, dishwasher casing, and the wall cabinet. Also think about the flooring for this wet area, a splashback behind the sink to protect the walls, task lighting, and curtains.

△ LIGHT FITTINGS
Work out a lighting plan and sort out the wiring before the kitchen is installed. Attach light fittings when the room is almost finished.

▷ FLOOR PLAN
A bird's eye view shows you exactly how the kitchen elements are placed in relation to the shape of the room.

△ ❸ FIXED FEATURES
Plot fixed features, such as the built-in cupboard and window, to check how much space is available for a table and chairs in front of these features. Draw the dishwasher stack in profile to ensure the cupboard doors can open fully without any obstruction.

FABRICS AND FINISHES ▷
When planning your budget, allow money for finishing decoration and furnishings. Quality curtain fabrics and wood cabinet finishes add extra comfort and warmth to the kitchen.

WHAT NEXT?

■ Take your finished design to a major kitchen manufacturer, a specialist kitchen design company, or a local cabinet maker. They can check your plans and provide technical information.

■ Obtain permission from relevant authorities for any structural alterations.

■ The coordination of the work is important. Agree a schedule with the builders, plumbers, electricians, fitters, and decorators involved. The order of work is as follows: structural alterations; wiring and plumbing; floor-laying; base-coat decoration; cabinet-fitting, and then the final electrical, plumbing, and decoration work.

■ Check that the delivery dates for appliances, cabinets, and materials meet your work schedule.

■ When you know how long the job will take, set up a temporary kitchen or make other eating arrangements.

BUDGET TIPS

■ After producing your initial design, work out how much appliances, cabinets, flooring and other materials will cost. Obtain estimates for building, plumbing, and electrical work that needs to be done to help you calculate the costs of installing your new kitchen.

■ If your ideal kitchen design is beyond your budget, see where you can cut expenditure. Perhaps you can reduce the scale of building work, select less expensive flooring and worktops, and use fewer quality cabinets.

■ Allow some contingency in the budget to cover unexpected costs that may arise.

STOCKISTS AND SUPPLIERS

The following directory of useful names and addresses will help you source the specialist kitchen shops needed to furnish and equip your brand-new kitchen. The letters (MO) after an entry indicate that items are only available by mail order; some retailers may operate a mail order service as well as selling through a shop (Also available MO).

KITCHEN OUTFITTERS

ALTERNATIVE PLANS
9 Hester Road
London SW11 4AN
Tel: 0171 228 6460
Suppliers of stylish Italian kitchens, including Boffi.

ARC LINEA OF KNIGHTSBRIDGE
164 Brompton Road
London SW3 1HW
Tel: 0171 581 2271
Top-of-the-range Italian-designed fitted kitchens.

ARENA
Bartlemas Farmhouse
Bartlemas
Oxfordshire OX4 2AJ
Tel: 01865 726505
Handmade traditional kitchens.

B&Q PLC (HEAD OFFICE)
Portswood House
1 Hampshire Corporate Park
Chandler's Ford
Eastleigh
Hampshire SO5 3YX
Tel: 0181 466 4166 for details of local stores.
Low-cost kitchen units.

BULTHAUP
37 Wigmore Street
London W1H 9LD
Tel: 0171 495 3663
Sophisticated German kitchen design.

CHALON
The Plaza
535 King's Road
London SW10 OSZ
Tel: 0171 351 0008
Unfitted painted wood kitchens.

C.P. HART & SONS LTD
Newnham Terrace
Hercules Road
London SE1 7DR
Tel: 0171 902 1000
Top European kitchen and bathroom furniture. (Also available MO)

CRABTREE KITCHENS
The Twickenham Centre
Norcutt Road
Twickenham
Middlesex TW2 6SR
Tel: 0181 755 1121
Handcrafted traditional and contemporary kitchens.

EMPEROR KITCHENS LTD
Capricorn House
5 Birchall Street
Liverpool L20 8PD
Tel: 0151 944 1825
Fitted interior specialists using unusual woods.

HOUSEWORKS LTD
11–15 Upper Erne Street
Dublin 2
Republic of Ireland
Tel: 003531 6769511
Stockists of Siematic kitchens.

IKEA LTD
Ikea Tower
255 North Circular Road
London NW10 OJQ
Tel: 0181 233 2300 for details of local stores.
Lost-cost kitchens with design flair.

JOHNNY GREY & CO
Fyning Copse
Rogate
Petersfield
Hampshire GU31 5DH
Tel: 01730 821424
Individually designed kitchens and interior architecture.

MARK QUINN-WILSON
5 Eastport Lane
Lewes
East Sussex BN7 1TL
Tel: 01273 471913
Hand-built kitchens, mostly made from old pine.

MOWLEM & CO
3a Clayton Road
Jesmond
Newcastle upon Tyne NE2 4RP
Tel: 0191 281 3443
Handmade wood kitchens and kitchens for the disabled.

NEWCASTLE FURNITURE COMPANY
128 Walham Green Court
Moore Park Road
London SW6 4DG
Tel: 0171 386 9203
Simple Shaker-style furniture for kitchens.

NICHOLAS ANTHONY
40 Wigmore Street
London W1H 9DF
Tel: 0171 935 0177
Suppliers of high-quality fitted kitchens.

ORM KITCHENS
11–15 Erne Street
Dublin 2
Republic of Ireland
Tel: 003531 6769511
Low-cost country kitchens.

PLAIN ENGLISH DESIGN LTD
The Tannery
Combs
Stowmarket
Suffolk IP14 2EN
Tel: 01449 774028
Units in the National Trust range of colours.

POGGENPOHL
Silbury Court
368 Silbury Boulevard
Central Milton Keynes
Buckinghamshire MK9 2AF
Tel: 01908 606886 for stockists.
Quality German fitted kitchens.

ROBINSON AND CORNISH LTD
Southay House
Oakwood Close
Roundswell
Barnstaple
Devon EX31 3NJ
Tel: 01271 329300
Traditional English fitted kitchens.

SIEMATIC MÖBELWERK GMBH & CO
Osprey House
Rookery Court
Primett Road
Stevenage
Hertfordshire SG1 3EE
Tel: 01438 369327
Quality fitted kitchens.

MARK WILKINSON
Overton House
High Street
Bromham
Nr Chippenham
Wiltshire SN15 2HA
Tel: 01380 850004
*Quality English fitted and
unfitted kitchens.*

ZEYKO UK LTD
14 Chequers Street
St. Albans
Hertfordshire AL1 3YB
Tel: 01727 835500 for stockists.
Pale wood kitchen units.

KITCHEN APPLIANCES

AGA-RAYBURN
PO Box 30
Ketley
Telford TF1 4DD
Tel: 0345 125207
Manufacturers of cooking ranges.

AMERICAN APPLIANCE CENTRE
19 Mill Lane
Woodford Green
Essex IG8 OUN
Tel: 0181 506 2039
*Suppliers of American-style fridges, cooking
ranges, and other kitchen appliances.*

ATAG UK
19 Hither Green
Clevedon
Somerset BS21 6XU
Tel: 01275 877301
Manufacturers of built-in appliances.

BOSCH DOMESTIC APPLIANCES LTD
Old Wolverton Road
Wolverton
Milton Keynes
Buckinghamshire MK12 5PT
Tel: 0181 573 1199
Manufacturers of kitchen appliances.

GAGGENAU UK LTD
Contract Kitchen Projects
G2 Chelsea Design Centre
Chelsea Harbour
London SW10 0XE
Tel: 0171 352 2155
Manufacturers of appliances.

IMPERIAL UK
Fairacres
Marcham Road
Abingdon
Oxfordshire OX14 1TW
Tel: 01235 554455
*Manufacturers of kitchen
appliances, including steam
ovens. (Imperial UK is a
division of Miele.)*

IN-SINK-ERATOR DIVISION
Chelmsford Road
Great Dunmow
Essex CM6 1LP
Tel: 01371 873073
*Suppliers of electrically operated
rubbish compactors.*

LEON JAEGGI & SONS LTD
77 Shaftesbury Avenue
London W1V 7AD
Tel: 0171 434 4545 for further details.
*Suppliers of professional heavy-duty cookers
and catering appliances and equipment.*

MIELE COMPANY
Fairacres
Marcham Road
Abingdon
Oxfordshire OX14 1TW
Tel: 01235 554455
*Manufacturers of kitchen appliances, including
steam ovens. (Imperial UK is a division of Miele.)*

NEFF UK LTD
The Quadrangle
Westmount Centre
Uxbridge Road
Hayes
Middlesex UB4 OHD
Tel: 0181 848 3711
*Appliance manufacturer.
(Catalogue available on 0800 318372)*

OLD TOWN
32 Elm Hill
Norwich
Norfolk NR3 1HG
Tel: 01603 628100
*Stockists of enamelled cookers
and fridges from 1940s.*

SMEG UK LTD
Corinthian Court
80 Milton Park
Abingdon
Oxfordshire OX14 4RY
Tel: 01235 861090
Manufacturers of appliances.

TREMBATH DISTRIBUTORS
Felstead Road
Longmead Industrial Est.
Epsom
Surrey KT19 9XS
Tel: 01372 745745
UK distributor of Jenn-Air ovens and hobs.

KITCHEN EQUIPMENT

BELOW STAIRS
103 High Street
Hungerford
Berkshire RG17 0NB
Tel: 01488 682317
*Traditional kitchen accessories,
including bread crocks.*

BODUM UK
24 Neal Street
London WC2H 9PS
Tel: 0171 240 9176
Modern kitchen equipment. (Also available MO)

THE CONRAN SHOP
Michelin House
81 Fulham Road
London SW3 6RD
Tel: 0171 589 7401
*Fashionably modern kitchen accessories
and utensils. (Also available MO)*

LA CUISINIERE
81–83 Northcote Road
London SW11 6PJ
Tel: 0171 223 4487
*Extensive range of kitchen equipment.
(Also available MO)*

DAVID MELLOR
4 Sloane Square
London SW1W 8EE
Tel: 0171 730 4259
*State-of-the-art kitchenware and cutlery.
(Also available MO)*

DIVERTIMENTI
139–141 Fulham Road
London SW3 6SD

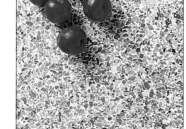

Tel: 0171 581 8065
*Wide selection of kitchen
equipment. (Also available
MO on 0171 386 9911)*

ENGLISH HURDLE
Curload
Stoke St. Gregory
Taunton
Somerset TA3 6JD
Tel: 01823 698418
*English kitchen basketware,
mostly made to order.*

GRAHAM & GREEN
4, 7, & 10 Elgin Crescent
London W11 2JA
Tel: 0171 727 4594
*Mixture of wood, wrought-iron, garden and
kitchen furniture, accessories, and kitchen
equipment. (Also available MO)*

HOGARTH & DWYER
240 High Street
Guildford
Surrey GU1 3JF
Tel: 01483 456250
*High-quality kitchen equipment.
(Also available MO on 01249 449149)*

JERRY'S HOME STORE
163–167 Fulham Road
London SW3 6SN
Tel: 0171 225 2246
*American kitchen equipment.
(Also available MO on 0171 581 0909)*

KITCHEN COMPLEMENTS
Chatham Street
Dublin 2
Republic of Ireland
Tel: 003531 6770734
Range of kitchen equipment. (Also available MO)

MICHAEL LEWIS
16 Essex Road
London N1 8LN
Tel: 0171 359 7733
1940s enamelled kitchenware.

STAINES CATERING
15–19 Brewer Street
London W1R 3FL
Tel: 0171 437 8424
*Reasonably priced basic kitchen equipment.
(Also available MO)*

THE SUMMER HOUSE
3–5 Waterloo Square
Alfriston
East Sussex BN26 5UD
Tel: 01323 870356
*Spanish ceramic plates, jugs, and kitchenware.
(Also available MO)*

SUMMERHILL AND BISHOP
100 Portland Road
London W11 4LN
Tel: 0171 221 4566
*Kitchen accessories from North Africa,
Portugal, and France.*

KITCHEN SINKS AND FITTINGS

ARMITAGE SHANKS LTD
Armitage
Nr Rugeley
Staffordshire WS15 4BT
Tel: 01543 490253 for stockists.
Traditional white Belfast sinks.

BLANCO LTD
Oxgate Lane
London NW2 7JN
Tel: 0181 450 9100 for stockists.
Wide range of products in varying price ranges.

BRASS AND TRADITIONAL SINKS LTD
Devauden Green
Chepstow
Monmouthshire NP6 6PL
Tel: 01291 650738
*Wide choice of traditional and
modern sinks and taps.*

FRANKE UK LTD
East Park
M.I.O.C.
Styal Road
Manchester M22 5WB
Tel: 0161 436 6280 for stockists.
*Extensive selection of fittings at a range of prices,
including high-quality stainless steel taps.*

LEISURE GLYNWED LTD
Meadow Lane
Long Eaton
Nottingham NG10 2AT
Tel: 0115 9464000
*Wide range of round or square sinks
in stainless steel and resin.*

PLAND STAINLESS
Lower Wortley Ring Road
Leeds LS12 6AA
Tel: 0113 263 4184
*Wide range of stainless steel
sinks and units.*

WALLCOVERINGS, WORKTOPS, AND FLOORINGS

AMTICO
The Amtico Showroom
18 Hanover Square
London W1R 9BD
Tel: 0171 629 6258
Wide choice of flooring materials.

ANCHOR FOOD SERVICE EQUIPMENT
205 Manor Road
Erith
Kent DA8 2AD
Tel: 01322 335544
Stainless steel worktops and units.

BALDWIN PLASTIC LAMINATES LTD
57 Tallon Road
Hutton Industrial Estate
Brentwood
Essex CM13 1TG
Tel: 01277 225235
Plastic laminates in bright colours.

BROOKS GROUP LTD
27 Duncrue Street
Belfast
Northern Ireland
BT3 9AR
Tel: 01232 2744201
Quality hardwood floors.

DELABOLE SLATE
Pengelly Road
Delabole
Cornwall PL33 9AZ
Tel: 01840 212242
Slate worktop tiles.

DESIGNERS GUILD
267–271 & 275–277 King's Road
London SW3 5EN
Tel: 0171 243 7300
*Hand-painted, brightly coloured
wallpapers and fabrics.*

DOMUS TILES
33 Parkgate Road
London SW11 4NP
Tel: 0171 223 5555
High-quality Italian tiles, mostly machine-made.

FIRED EARTH PLC
Twyford Mill
Oxford Road
Adderbury
Oxfordshire OX17 3HP
Tel: 01295 812088
*Terracotta, mosaic, and marble,
and handmade ceramic tiles for
floors and walls.*

FORMICA LTD
Coast Road
North Shields
Tyne and Wear NE29 8RE
Tel: 0191 259 3000
*Manufacturer of plastic
laminates.*

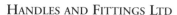

FROYLE TILES LTD
Froyle Pottery
Lower Froyle
Alton
Hampshire GU34 4LL
Tel: 01420 23693
*Handmade tiles in a wide
range of colours, to order.*

GEC ANDERSON
89 Hercomer Road
Bushy
Hertfordshire WD2 3LS
Tel: 0181 950 1826
Manufacturers of stainless steel worktops, to order.

GLACIEN GLASS LTD
129 Church Walk
London N16 8QW
Tel: 0181 254 8752
Acid-etched glass.

JUNCKERS
Wheaton Court
Commercial Centre
Wheaton Road
Witham
Essex CM8 3UJ
Tel: 01376 517512
Suppliers of quality wood floors.

LIVRA
Arch 8
Culvert Place
London SW11 5BA
Tel: 0171 627 3600
Suppliers of granite and marble worktops.

LLOYD OF BEDWYN
91 Church Street
Great Bedwyn
Marlborough
Wiltshire SN8 3PF
Tel: 01672 870234
Granite and slate worktops.

MILLAND FINE TIMBERS LTD
Iping Road
Milland
near Liphook
Hampshire GU30 7MA
Tel: 01428 741344
Floors and worktops.

PALLAM PRECAST
187 West End Lane
London NW6 1SR
Tel: 0171 328 6512
Made-to-measure terrazzo worktops.

PARIS CERAMICS
583 King's Road
London SW6 2EH
Tel: 0171 371 7778
*High-quality floor and wall tiles
in limestone and terracotta.*

SINCLAIR TILL
791 Wandsworth Road
London SW8 3JQ
Tel: 0171 720 0031
*Handcut linoleums and wood
flooring in modern colours and shapes.*

KITCHEN FURNITURE

RJ's HOMESHOP
209 Tottenham Court Road
London W1P 9AF
Tel: 0171 637 7474
Low-cost kitchen furniture.

VIADUCT FURNITURE LTD
1–10 Summers Street
London EC1R 5BD
Tel: 0171 278 8456
*Top Italian, French, and Spanish designer
dining tables and chairs.*

HABITAT (HEAD OFFICE)
196 Tottenham Court Road
London W1P 9LD
Tel: 0171 255 2545
Good selection of kitchen furniture.

KITCHEN LIGHTING

CONCORD LIGHTING LTD
174 High Holborn
London WC1V 7AA
Tel: 0171 497 1400
A wide range of modern lighting equipment.

CONNECT LIGHTING
Murrils Estate
East Street
Portchester
Fareham
Hampshire PO16 9RD
Tel: 01705 375140
*Lighting equipment to order.
Low-voltage fittings specialists.*

FUTIMIS LTD
11 Mead Industrial Park
River Way
Harlow
Essex CM20 2SE
Tel: 01279 411131
*High-quality lighting
equipment.*

HANDLES AND FITTINGS LTD
Haf House
Mead Lane
Hertford
Hertfordshire SG13 7AP
Tel: 01992 505655
Handles, ironmongery, electrical switchplates.

HEALS
196 Tottenham Court Road
London W1P 9LD
Tel: 0171 636 1666
Range of contemporary light fittings.

THE LIGHT STORE
11 Clifton Road
London W9 1SZ
Tel: 0171 286 0233
*Wide range of domestic lighting
equipment.*

LONDON LIGHTING COMPANY
135 Fulham Road
London SW3 2RT
Tel: 0171 589 3612
Good selection of light fittings for the home.

NATIONAL LIGHTING SHOWROOM
11–15 Upper Erne Street
Dublin 2
Republic of Ireland
Tel: 003531 6769555
Variety of lighting supplies.

WANDSWORTH ELECTRICAL LTD
Albert Drive
Sheerwater
Woking
Surrey GU21 5SE
Tel: 01483 740740
Good selection of electrical lighting equipment.

SPECIALIST PAINTERS

FELIX DELMAR
The Valley Farm
Lamarsh
Nr. Bures
Suffolk CO8 5EZ
Tel: 01787 269819
Murals, abstracts, and friezes.

LUCY TURNER
c/o Johnny Grey & Co.
Fyning Copse
Rogate
Petersfield
Hampshire GU31 5DH
Tel: 01730 821424
Friezes, panels, and borders.

INDEX

ACKNOWLEDGMENTS

AUTHOR'S ACKNOWLEDGMENTS

I would like to thank all those who allowed us into their homes to photograph their kitchens, particularly my clients Nick and Joan Marmont, Nick and Susie Ussiskin, and my wife Becca, and in addition, Mr and Mrs Miles, Julia and Nick Parker, and also Mark and Sara Quinn-Wilson.

Special gratitude is due to the craftsmen with whom I've worked over the years, their skill, spirit, and hard work turning my kitchen ideas into beautifully made furniture. They include, amongst many others, Jonathan Morriss, Stephen Cordell, Gordon Hopkins, Jonathan Parlett, Miles Muggleton, Andrew Parslow, Nigel Brown, Patrick Warnes, Paul Jobst, Paul Saban, John Barnard and Robin Weeks, specialist painters Jenny Holt, Felix Delmar, and the artist Lucy Turner.

My own design team too, deserve much credit for their hard work and enthusiasm – David Richards, Lynne Fornieles, Mike Rooke, Will Jameson, Anna Moore, and Richard Lee who also conceived the beautifully detailed kitchen illustrations that feature throughout the book.

I owe a special thanks to the team at Dorling Kindersley. First of all to Mary-Clare Jerram and Amanda Lunn who persuaded me to write the book, to Colin Walton who designed it so carefully and provided art direction, and to my brave editor Bella Pringle, who deserves a great deal of credit for her hard work and skill. Many thanks also to photographer Peter Anderson for his careful eye, his patience, and his hard work.

Finally, heartfelt thanks to my wife who put up with my absence at crucial periods of family life, to allow me the time to write two books at once, and still provide encouragement when needed.

PUBLISHER'S ACKNOWLEDGMENTS

Dorling Kindersley would also like to thank: Rebecca and Johnny Grey, Nick and Joan Marmont, Mr and Mrs Miles, Julia and Nick Parker, Nick and Susie Ussiskin, and Mark and Sara Quinn-Wilson for allowing us to photograph their kitchens.

Thank you also to the following kitchen showrooms who granted us permission to photograph on their premises: Arc Linea; Bulthaup; Chalon; C.P. Hart; Newcastle Furniture Company; Nicholas Anthony, and to Fired Earth, for use of their floorings.

We are also grateful to those who kindly supplied props: American Appliance Centre; Amtico; Christoph Caffyn; La Cuisinière; David Mellor; Formica Ltd; Geneviève Lethu; Graham & Green; Hogarth & Dwyer; Jerry's Home Store; Mediterranean Imports; Moore Park Delicatessen; Pallam Precast; P.G. Kitchens & Bathrooms; RJ's HomeShop; Sinclair Till, and Viaduct Furniture Ltd.

Special thanks also goes to: Jeremy Myerson for helping us to establish this series, Phillip Hayes, UK managing director of Siematic kitchens, for his time and helpful advice; to Charlotte Davies and Clive Hayball for their guidance throughout the project; to Angeles Gavira and Simon Maughan for editorial assistance; to Ann Kay for proof-reading; and to Hilary Bird for the index.

ARTWORK: Richard Lee

PHOTOGRAPHY:
All photographs by Peter Anderson and Matthew Ward except:
(Kitchen designers are named in brackets.)
Peter Aprahamian (Johnny Grey) 10, 52–53; Interior Archive / Tim Beddow

(John Pawson) 56bl; Simon Brown (Johnny Grey) 57; Michael Focard (Johnny Grey) 65; Ray Main 8bl, 52tl, and 52bl, 60tl, 61, 64tr; Diana Miller 8t, 37tr, 85t; James Mortimer (Johnny Grey) 6b; David Parmiter (Claudia Bryant) 52br, 56tr and 56br; Colin Radcliffe Design 64bl; Trevor Richards (Johnny Grey) 6, 9, 40cl, 64tl and 64br, 72br; Paul Ryan / International Interiors (Fell-Clark Design) 68bl; Paul Ryan / International Interiors (Gerry Nelisson) 68br; Deidi von Schaewen 68tl; Fritz von der Schulenberg (Nico Rensch) 46cl; Colin Walton 40bl, 43tr, 76br, 77tr, 78–79b, 80tl, 87b.

The following companies kindly lent us their photographs: Aga-Rayburn 13tl, 30t; Alternative Plans 37b; Chalon 56bl; Jenn-Air (CV4380PG) 28t, (WW27210PG) 31bl, (SVD8310PG) 82; John Lewis of Hungerford 72tr; Kohler 27b; Newcastle Furniture Company 56tl; Snaidero 52cb; Sub-zero 20bl; Wrighton Kitchens 'Albany' (Texas Homecare and selected Homebase stores) 44l.

Every effort has been made to trace the copyright holders. We apologise for any unintentional omission and would be pleased to insert these in subsequent editions.

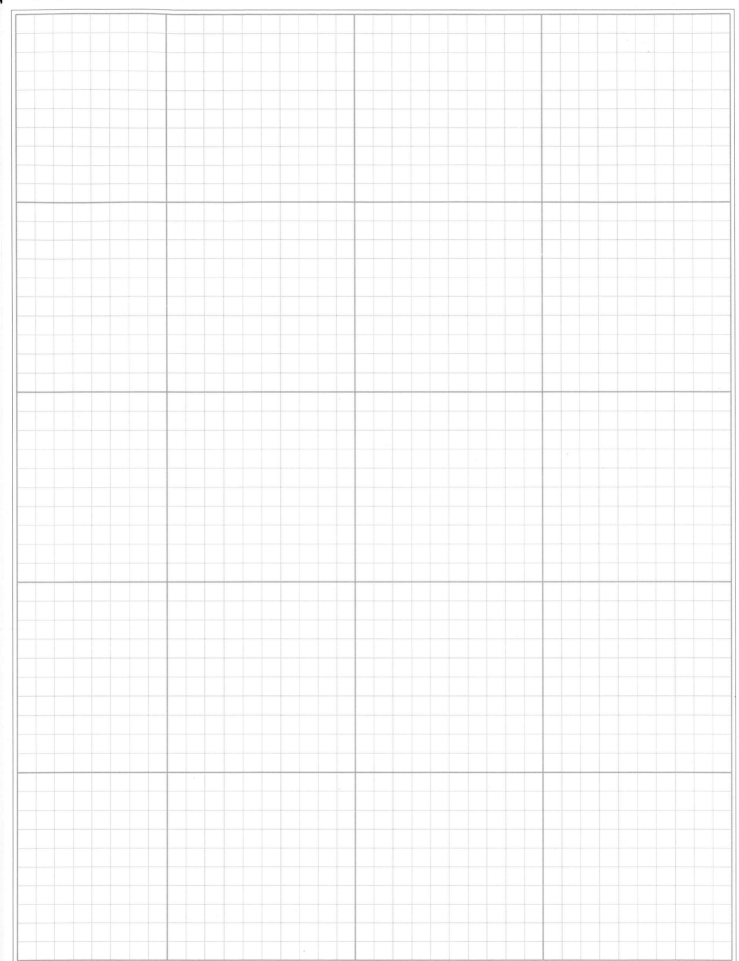

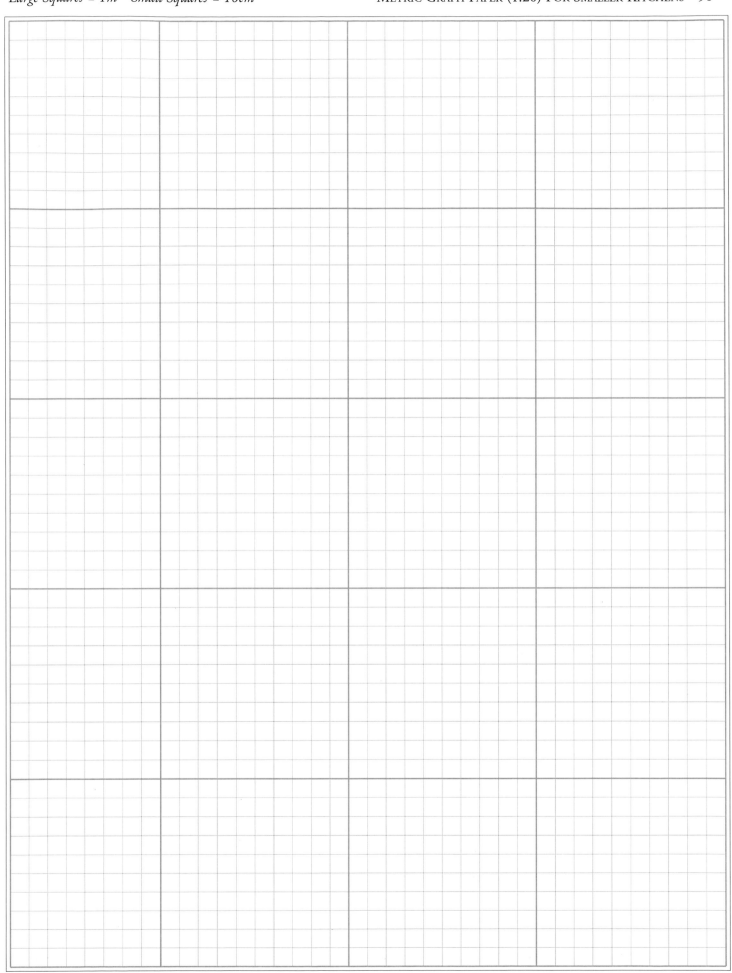

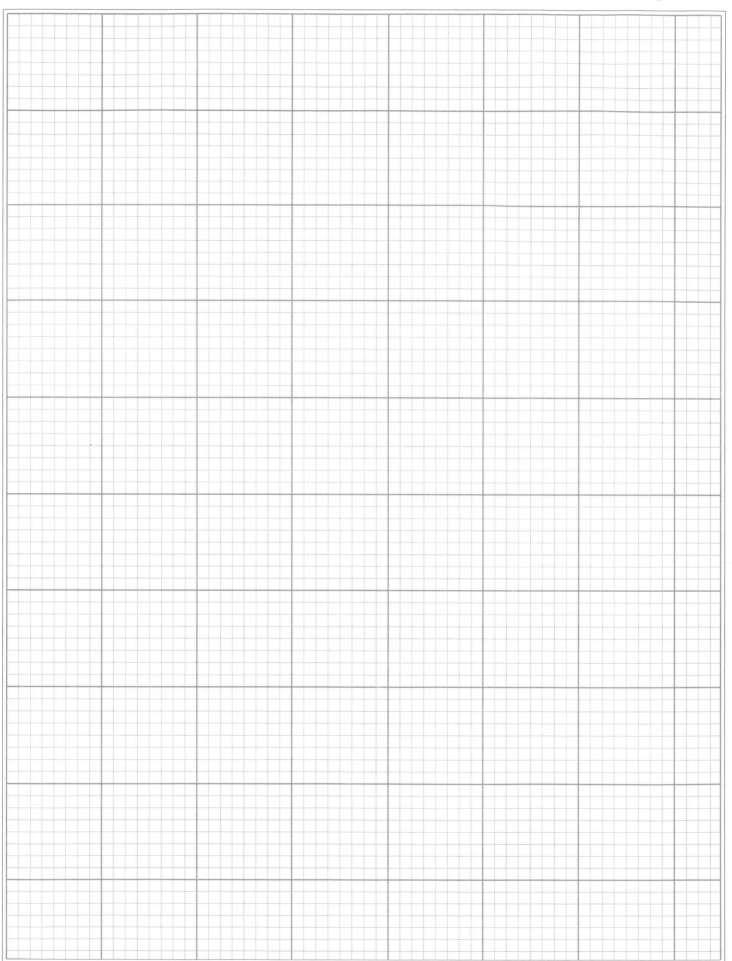

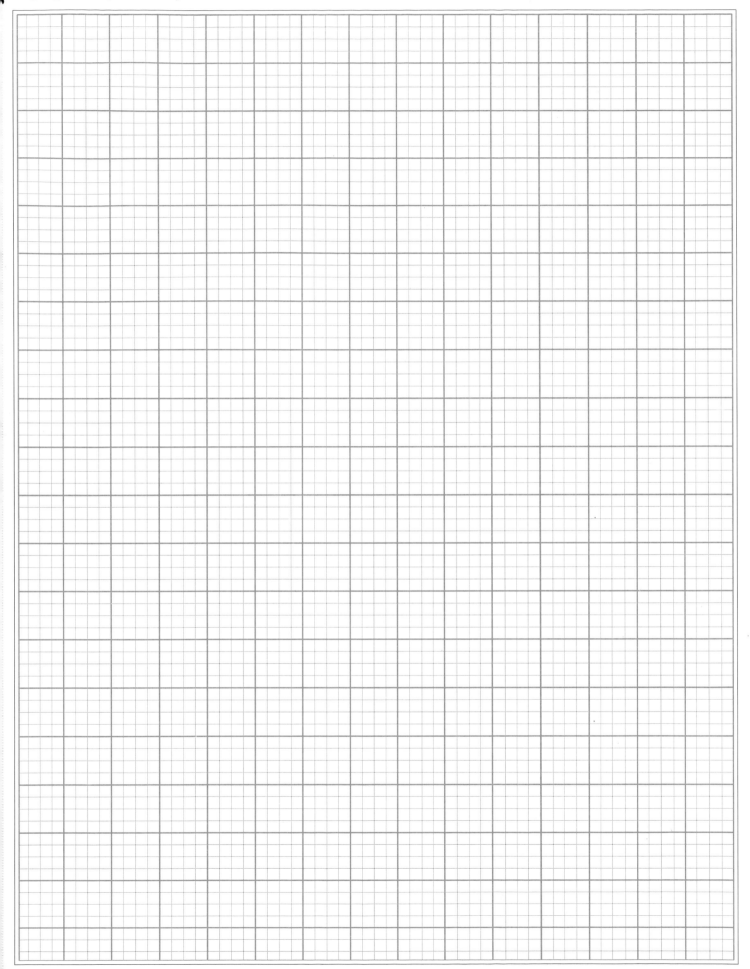

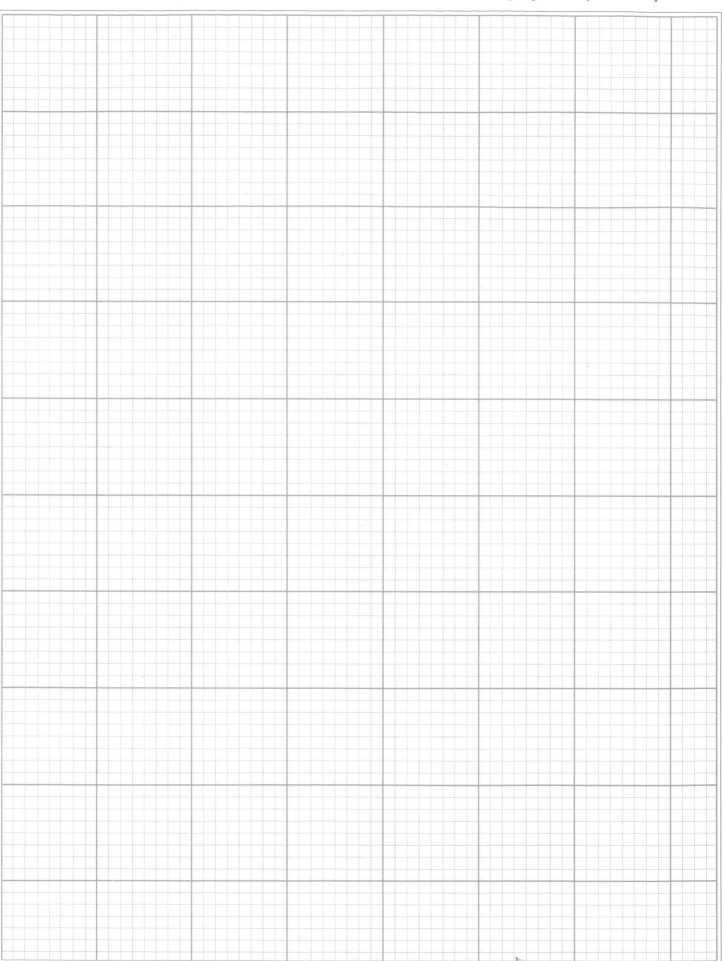